PⅬ

by

Discovery Retail Group

© 2019 Philip H. Mitchell & Gary A. Petz

(888) 292-6531

Published

2019

Advance Praise
For
Stores on Fire
A Retailer's Story

"Stores on Fire" is a breath of fresh air in a category flooded with "how-to" and lecture style texts. Philip and Gary take us on an adventure with a relatable store owner who finds himself in many familiar situations to us in the retail industry. As a longtime user of Discovery Retail Group's "Profit Explorer," reading this book has a compounding benefit to our company and an enjoyable nudge along the path of productivity.

Alex Porter
Vice President of Operations
Porters Building Centers

The latest collaboration from Phil Mitchell and Gary Petz provides the reader with an enjoyable and genuine guide to retail improvement. You will appreciate Charlie Kern's transformation from a depressed store owner to a passionate community leader with his new skills. "Stores on Fire" is a great book to share with your associates to start building a better team. Home Lumber has benefitted from their retail insight and enthusiasm for over a decade now. Keep the contributions coming you two!

John Humphreys
President
Home Lumber and Supply

Advance Praise
For
Stores on Fire
A Retailer's Story

I loved "Stores on Fire". The format makes it an easy read and the content is great common sense stuff that actually applies to the day to day operations of a Home Center. It is obvious this book was written by people who have worked in (and been successful in) our industry. I plan to get copies of "Stores on Fire" into the hands of our key employees as soon as it's available.

Jonathan Kennedy
President and General Manager
The T.H. Rogers Lumber Company

I had the privilege of attending the NRHA Executive management course. Several of the successful improvement plans for our company came from adapting ideas garnered from Discovery Retail Group.

This book, Stores on Fire, was an enjoyable easy read and delivered many key points on business improvements. The book shared ideas in such a way as to give the reader a blueprint for what they could do in their own store.

Randy Ostrom
Senior Store Manager
Buchheit Stores, Greenville and Centralia

Advance Praise
For
Stores on Fire
A Retailer's Story

"Stores on Fire" is a great book for anyone working in the Hardware/Home Center industry regardless of your position. There are great retail tips that even the most successful stores in the industry can execute to drive top line sales and bottom line profits. I strongly encourage anyone in the Hardware/Home Center Industry to read this masterpiece written by Gary and Phil.

Josiah Gates
Vice President
Aubuchon Hardware

Philip & Gary strike again by weaving proven business principles into an enjoyable and compelling narrative that strikes at the heart of the independent hardware industry! I found myself saying "this is what we look like and we can make the same changes to improve our business!" Get everyone in your company to read it!

Jim Hostetter
President
PaulB Hardware & PaulB Wholesale

Advance Praise
For
Stores on Fire
A Retailer's Story

With their new book, Stores on Fire, Phil Mitchel and Gary Petz have captured the key questions and concerns that keep so many independent retailers up at night. The protagonist could be any independent retailer in any community, perplexed by a lack of sales, profits and the energy to continue searching for solutions. But then a glimmer of hope … from a fellow retailer who shares not a quick fix, but a proven, time-tested method for growing sales and profits. The ensuing journey takes the reader through a deep review of the many details of retail of which some are art, and others science.

Stores on Fire and its companion workbook are both inspirational and aspirational. Based on the Incremental Improvement System that Mitchel and Petz teach students in NRHA's Retail Management Certification Program, its story will ring true and familiar, while its practices, processes and procedures will re-energize the vitality and viability of any retail operation. It's yet another "must-read" for all independent retailers from Mitchel and Petz.

Scott Wright, Executive Director—Retail Leadership Institute

North American Retail Hardware Association

Chapter 1

I won't lie to you; it was good to get away from home for a while. Good to get away from the store and, as bad as it may sound, good to get away from Julie, too. Don't get me wrong, I sympathized with her, and I tried to understand her feelings. But the wreck that killed her parents, my in-laws, had happened nearly three years earlier and she was still reliving the loss every day.

First you need to understand that it was more than just the sudden loss of her parents. That alone would have been traumatic enough to deal with. But, as I said, it's more than that. Julie and I left Indianapolis, pulled up stakes, and left steady jobs to join her parents in Springston, Missouri. They had purchased a home center there eight or nine years earlier. It was their intention to revive the struggling operation. They called us about four years later and said the store was growing and that business was better. They went on to say that they were hoping to slow down over the next few years and that they would love for us to learn the business. They felt it would provide a good life for Julie and me in a town that "would be perfect for raising children." We didn't have children at the time, but they were right in one regard, Springston would be a great community to grow up in.

So, Julie and I, after many hours of discussion, made the decision to take them up on their offer. We both felt that Julie should continue to work outside the business, and thank God she did. We learned after the fact that although business at the home center was improving it was far from lucrative and would not provide us the lifestyle we wanted. Julie set up a hair salon, which had always been her dream. Her business grew slowly and having something to occupy her mind was a godsend.

A little less than a year after we got here, Julie called me, sobbing uncontrollably. A highway patrol officer had stopped and broke the news to her about the accident that claimed the lives of her parents. Jack and Melinda had left me in charge at the store for a few days. They needed a break and were going to attend a trade show. Just twenty miles outside of Chicago, where the show was held, their car was hit head-on by another vehicle whose driver had fallen asleep. Jack, Melinda and the other gentleman all died at the scene.

I hurried home to try and console her but, of course, she was too distraught to see anything other than the obvious loss. For weeks she cried most days, and I understood, at least, I tried to. But there we were, almost three years later, and still even the smallest discussion, and particularly any time we had conflict, she would begin to cry. When the crying started, I disengaged. She had never been like that before.

While I was at work one day, at about that time, my mom called to tell me that she needed to have some surgery. It wasn't serious she assured, but surgery nonetheless. She and dad retired to Florida a few years back, and I could tell she wanted me there for the operation. I would be there for the surgery, I told her, but I would need to be back soon. She understood and appreciated it. The procedure went great. So, at least for a time, that was off my mind.

Here I was, driving home, enjoying the windshield time and thinking about my situation. The business was not doing great, and that's a huge understatement. It was barely breaking even. Honestly, I had no idea how to improve it. Jack and Melinda had made some progress, but it hadn't been enough. And when I was forced to take over the operation after being there for less than a year, the store slid backwards. I'll admit that I was already thinking about how I might bail on the commitment. But Julie wouldn't hear of it. The business had meant a lot to her mother and her dad particularly, so she was not willing to accept failure. That's all well and good, except it left me trying to figure things out.

So, as I said, I was driving home and I come up on this town, Freemont, Arkansas, population 17,000 and something. That's a coincidence, I thought, because it was almost the same size as Springston. The town didn't look bad. I figured Springston looked better, but I can't really say why, maybe a bit cleaner, I don't know. Then, on my right, I saw it: Miller Home Center. Wow! What a great looking operation. It wasn't a new building but it looked awesome. It was up to date and very attractive. It had modern lines, was well identified and clean. The parking lot was dark and smooth; parking lines clearly visible, and most importantly, the parking lot was full. I slowed down a bit to take it all in. I felt a twinge of jealousy. No, wait a minute; scratch that! I felt a lot jealous as I drove by.

Call it serendipity, blind luck or divine intervention, I don't know, but here's what happened next. Less than two miles up the same highway there was another Home Center. This one told a different story. In many ways it reminded me of Chard's Home Center. Did I mention that's what Jack had named the store he bought? Well anyway the two operations, mine and this one, looked a lot alike. The weird thing was I recognized that this store looked like it was in death throes. I found myself wondering if that was what the public saw when they looked at our store.

You're not given too many ah-ha moments in life, but right then I had an epiphany. I realized I had to go back and talk to the owner of that amazing looking store, if he or she would see me. For sure though, I knew I had to try.

Bat turn!

Stores on Fire

Chapter 2

It didn't take too long to get back to Miller Home Center, and I've got to tell you that I almost chickened out about going in. I didn't want to just look around. I've been in nice stores before. No, I was going in for the specific purpose of trying to pick the brain of the owner or manager. I was going to be up front about why I was there and just gauge the reaction. It felt weird, but I was also feeling a tad desperate. At the time I didn't know that this simple choice would change the trajectory of our store.

I walked into the vestibule and was instantly impressed with how the interior reflected the same attention to detail as the exterior. Back home we try to keep our store pretty clean, but I swear this place was operating at a completely different level. When I stepped into the showroom I was surprised by how different the layout was. The gondolas were not lined up like church pews, you know the way you see them in most home centers, and the way they were in our store. The main aisle angled off to the right and I followed it. The store was well lit, the temperature was perfect and there was pleasant music playing at a moderate volume level. I saw customers in many aisles and several clerks interacting with them.

When he noticed me a young man turned and smiled.

"Thanks for coming in, we'll be right with you. You working on anything special today?"

"No, I'm just kind of looking around," I replied.

"Great, I'll come and get acquainted when I finish here."

"I appreciate it," I said, not knowing any other way to react.

While he finished with his customer I continued walking deeper into the store. You know what surprised me? It seemed that I intuitively knew how to shop this store. That vague familiarity all seemed to be the by-product of the way it was arranged and signed. I really wouldn't have needed anyone to guide me to anything. There were large department signs that I could read from almost anywhere in the store. In the aisles there were category signs that made it easy to see what each aisle contained, as well as product location signs on the side counters at every six or eight feet. It was all very attractive. I was standing there thinking, "Wow these signs must have cost a pretty penny," when the young man approached.

"Hey, I'm Zack," he said, extending his hand, "Welcome to Miller Home Center. I'm glad you're here."

"Thanks, Zack, I'm Charley, Charley Kern," I said as we shook hands.

"You new around here, Charley? I don't remember seeing you before," Zack said, still smiling easily.

"Actually no, I'm just passing through. I was so impressed with the outside of your store that I wanted to see what it looked like on the inside."

"That's awesome, I'm glad you stopped. What do you think?"

"I'm very impressed. It's beautiful."

"Thanks," Zack said, "we're really proud of it."

"Oh, so you're an owner?" I asked.

Zack laughed out loud. "No, I just work here, but our whole team is proud of our store."

I wondered if any of my employees would have made a stranger feel this welcome and would have displayed this kind of pride in our operation, and I'm sorry to say I figured the answer was no.

Zack continued, "Danny Miller is the owner."

I asked, "Would he happen to be around?"

"I think so, but let me check for you. Did you need anything in particular, Charley?"

He had me.

I didn't really know what I was looking for or what I wanted for sure.

"Just wanted to meet him," I said. "I own a home center too, but please tell him that mine is located in Missouri and I'm not trying to steal any secrets." I smiled broadly hoping he wouldn't notice my lack of ease.

I guess it worked; he laughed and said, "OK, I'll tell him."

I continued to wander through the store, taking mental notes until Zack returned.

"Danny's with a customer. But he said he would love to meet you, and if you could drop back by around six, he'd buy you a beer."

I glanced at my watch. It was nearly 4:30 already. I had planned on driving home that night, but something in my gut told me that meeting Danny would be worth the wait.

"Yeah, I think I'll do that," I said. "I'll spend the night here. Where would you recommend I stay?"

"At the east end of town there's a nice place called The Meridian. It's clean, they do a good job and we furnished all the materials when they remodeled the place a few months ago," Zack said. "I'd be glad to give them a call to see if they have any vacancies."

"You know, I've got enough time," I said. "I'll just buzz out there and see. If they don't have any rooms, I noticed that there are other choices out that direction. You've been great, Zack. I appreciate it."

"No problem, Charley."

I left, wishing to myself that I had a few Zacks working my store.

***

I checked into the Meridian a few minutes later. Zack had steered me right. The place seemed clean, and the desk staff friendly.

"Zack, out at the Home Center suggested I stay with you guys," I offered.

The girl running the front desk smiled and replied, "Oh, nice. They're good people. I love to go in there. They make me feel important."

"You make it out there often?" I asked.

"I like to. I rent my place so I don't have much need for repair stuff, but I do go out there once in a while. They have some fun promotions on weekends, you know bar-b-cues, live music and games and such. A lot of people gather for their events. People here love their store."

An older lady in an adjacent office looked up from her work and over her reading glasses to join our conversation. "It sure is a far cry from what it used to be," she added. "It wasn't very good a few years ago, but Danny got it turned around, and I think they do real good now."

I nodded as I signed the receipt the girl had produced and pushed my way.

"Room 167," she said. "Park around on the south side and you'll be right there. I think you'll like the room. It's one of our bigger ones and has a nice view of the valley."

"Thanks," I replied. "I appreciate it."

The room was nice, and the clerk had been right—the view of the valley was extraordinary. Several pines reached to the sky interrupting an otherwise open meadow. The valley was dotted with several head of cattle. I wish I could have taken some time to drink it all in and enjoy the serenity, but I didn't have that luxury. I needed to be back to the store before long. I decided to give Julie a call first. After a few moments of catching up on her day I explained what I was doing and where I was staying.

"You sound kind of excited about it," she said.

"Do I?" I questioned myself as I pondered her statement. "Yeah, I guess I am. It should be interesting, and maybe I'll learn something."

"Boy, I sure hope so," she giggled. It reminded me of Julie the way she used to be.

A few moments later I fired up Clifford the big red truck and made my way back to Miller Home Center.

***

The parking lot at Miller Home Center was now nearly empty. The two vehicles that remained were parked along the side, so I assumed one belonged to Danny and the other to an employee. I parked out front. As I made my way to the vestibule I wondered how the place looked after dark. Maybe I would find out. The doors were locked, but I could see a lady closing the registers. I knocked on the glass. She looked up, smiled and made her way to open the door.

"You must be Charley," she said, southern accent and smiling warmly. "I'm Barb. Danny told me to watch for you."

"Looks like you're wrapping it up for the day," I said.

"Yep, it's been a good one, my gosh we were busy."

"That's good, right?"

"Oh, absolutely," she replied. "I hear you and Danny are going to grab a beer." Her smile grew as I nodded, "You better watch out for him, one usually doesn't do it."

She chuckled, amused at herself, before she continued. "I'll let him know you're here."

"I know he's here," someone said gruffly, "I heard you talking. What you trying to do, ruin my good reputation?" Danny was smiling broadly as he made his way up the aisle.

I learned, as time went along, that Danny wore a smile most of the time, and I must admit it was contagious.

"Hey, Danny, I'm Charley, thanks for taking time to meet me."

"No problem, man. I love talking shop," he said as he

extended a big paw.

Danny was a little overweight and not at all what I expected. He was mid to late forties. I guessed him at no more than five foot seven or so. He was dressed neatly but casually. I guess I thought he might be older and maybe taller. You know how you form mental images of someone before you meet them? I hadn't foreseen the paunch around his stomach which suggested he had met over beers more than a few times. Already we had something in common.

"I drove by your store today, and I was totally impressed. I came in and it looks great in here, too. I had to meet you."

"Thanks, man. I appreciate it. It wasn't always like this, let me assure you," he laughed easily.

"Really? I'd sure like to hear about that, maybe it would give me some hope." I imitated his smile. "I own a home center in Missouri, kind of inherited it actually. I'll tell you up front, it looks nothing like this, although I sure wish it did."

He laughed again. "Let me tell you brother, I hear what you're saying and I mean it when I say that this one was nothing like this a few years back, either." He made me feel very comfortable as he continued. "Come on, let's go grab dinner. I'll tell you some stories and who knows ... some of them might actually be true."

"Barb, you OK here? Alright if I go on?" he asked. I notice how he waited and seemed genuinely concerned about her answer.

"Sure, see you tomorrow, Dan."

Chapter 3

We stepped up into Danny's truck. It had high-lift springs, was polished, and looked very powerful.

"Tell you what," Danny said, "I'm going to take you to my favorite waterin' hole, Billy's Beach House."

"Billy's Beach House? Is it on a lake or something?" I asked.

"No." He said chuckling, "But from the name you'd think so, wouldn't you? No, Billy moved here from Florida a few years ago. He did some handyman work around for a while. That's how we got acquainted. He bought quite a bit of stuff from us back then and still buys some. Anyway, he got tired of that and decided to open this joint. Truth be told I didn't know if he would make it, didn't know if he had a big enough grub stake, if you know what I mean. But he's proved me wrong."

He paused as he guided the big Dodge into the parking lot. After finding a space and turning off the engine, he continued. "I enjoy the atmosphere and so do a lot of other people. It's all a matter of making them feel welcome and important, I guess." He thought a while longer and then added, "Well, that and the product, of course. Good burgers, cold drinks, and live music a couple times a week. It's all working pretty well. I think he kind of missed Florida though, so that's where the name came from. He wanted to recreate a little of the Keys' beach vibe. You ready to give it try?"

As we made our way in, six or eight people shouted welcomes to Danny. One approached and invited us to his table. Danny handled it.

"Thanks, Darrell, but my pal Charley and me are gonna be talking shop. I'll catch you next time. How about that?"

"OK" said the guy, "You playing Friday night?"

"Yeah, I'll be there. I want to thrash your butt again." Danny jeered.

The guy feigned surprise and shock. "We'll see, my man, we'll see." They laughed harmoniously.

Danny led the way to a booth near the back. "The music won't be as loud back here, I like Jimmy Buffet and all, but I want to be able to hear you." He motioned for me to sit.

"I'm having a Bud to start. What would you like?" he asked.

"I'll have the same," I answered.

"Hey April, when you get a chance bring us a couple Buds back here, would you?" Danny yelled out.

A trim, attractive blonde in short shorts and a t-shirt nodded, and a few moments later she placed two cold drafts on the table.

We talked football for a few minutes. He was knowledgeable and his love for the game shown through. Soon, however, Danny started the discussion that had brought us together, and I was all for it.

"So, tell me about your store," he said.

I told him about our moving to Springston and about the accident and our current situation. I described the store, and he nodded as if he could actually see what I described. He listened intently. There was never a time when I thought that he wasn't hanging on every word. I don't know if he had taken classes on listening or what, but he certainly seemed in-tune to what I was saying.

"Gosh, I'm sorry to hear about the accident. That must have been tough. Is your wife doing better?"

"Yeah it was hard. I think she's doing a little better." I said, recalling her laughter when we were on the phone earlier. "Truth is, the store is wearing on both of us now. It's a lot of pressure and it's a juggling act to just keep things afloat."

"So, what's your battle plan?" he said, staring at me intently.

I shrugged my shoulders. "I guess I just keep on trying, you know?"

"Trying what?"

"Trying to make things better," I said.

"But how? That's the point," he said, waiting for my response.

I don't know what I said immediately, but I remember a short time later I leveled with him. "I don't know, Danny, that's the problem."

He thought quietly for a moment, never removing his gaze and then finally asked. "Do you remember ever hearing the name, Sun Tzu?"

I thought for a moment trying to dig it out before saying, "I think I remember hearing it, but I don't remember where or why."

"He was a Chinese military strategist and philosopher, lived many years ago," he said. "His writings on warfare are still studied today in military and business academies and are considered to be premier writings on war strategies."

I smirked and said, "are we at war, Danny?"

This time he didn't return my smile, but slowly and seriously began to nod affirmation. "Yeah, brother, we are, and if you don't start viewing your situation as a battle, you're probably not going to do too much better than you're doing right now."

That was a depressing thought, and it sickened my stomach.

"So, why did you mention him?" I asked.

"I have a quote on my office wall," he said, "and I keep a copy in my billfold too. It's that important. I think it has a lot to do with why I find myself in the position I'm in today and not the one I was in six or seven years ago."

He rolled to one hip, reached and pulled out his billfold. "I want you to see it."

He located a piece of paper and passed it to me. I could tell he had carried it for a while and that it had probably been opened and folded many times. But, it was still easy to make it out. It read:

"Victorious warriors win first and then go to war, while defeated warriors go to war first and then seek to win"

He took a big gulp and then studied me. I could tell he wanted me to take something from the quote. But honestly, I had nothin'.

"OK, I'll bite," I said. "What does it mean, and why is it important?"

He was clearly passionate and jumped on my question. "It's warning against approaching business like you're trying to do it and like I was doing it. You're going to war every day without a strategy for improvement. You're going to war hoping things will get better. You need a battle plan. It may change after you initiate it, and that's fine. But you have to have a structure, processes and procedures for improvement."

I nodded while I considered what he had said. He sat quietly, reading me.

I finally offered, "Well, I'm working at cutting expenses."

He tilted his head and scratched the back of his neck. I thought he looked like he was carefully choosing his words.

"Listen, Danny," I said, "say it straight out. I'm a big boy. Your help may be my only opportunity."

He smiled. "OK, here you go. You're focusing on the wrong thing. You need to grow your business not prune it. I'm guessing you've cut expenses several times already. Am I right?"

I nodded.

"It's great when you're cuttin' fat," he said, but by this time you're probably cutting into muscle and you can't operate without muscle."

I'll admit that I may have missed Mr. Tzu's message, but this one hit me loud and clear.

Danny raised his hand and motioned for the server to bring us another drink.

"You guys eating?" She asked.

"Maybe later darlin'," Danny said.

***

"I understand what you're saying. Really, I do. But in my town there's a big box store at one end and you know how people are buying more stuff online all the time. So it makes sense to concentrate on cutting expenses. The way I see it, that's about all that I can do," I said.

Danny choked on the swallow he had just taken. It was probably because he had started to laugh at the same time he took a drink. His face turned red and his eyes looked wet.

"You ok?" I asked.

He raised his hand and nodded still trying to catch his breath. "Yeah, but you reminded me so much of my old man when you said that. He used to tell me that all the time."

"Tell you what?" I asked.

He continued to cough and chuckle for a while but then finally begin to relax having cleared the fluid from the wrong pipe. "Man you're killin' me here."

His eyes were still glassy from the choking episode but his smile remained. I thought to myself; I really like this guy.

He moved his head back and forth and began to speak again. "He started the store 30 years ago. He had a great run, and when he was younger he was a pretty good operator, I think. Anyway there was a point in time when he made a lot of money, I know that for sure. But by the time I came into the business he had lost his edge. It might have been his age, I don't know. What I do know is that he had made a fatal transition."

"Fatal transition, what do you mean?" I asked, hanging on every word now.

"Yeah, he stopped seeing possibilities, and when you get there, when you can no longer see possibilities, you're toast. So, I go into his office one day and I say, 'This place is tired, we need to reexamine where we are, where we're going and what it'll take to get there.'"

I saw a hint of pain or regret in Danny's face as he continued. "He got pissed and told me there was new competition, bigger stores and all that, and that we just couldn't hold our own. He said that we should just ride things out best we could. I flew off the handle and told him that I wished I would have known him back when he had some balls and when he wore a younger man's clothes."

Danny watched me raise my eyebrows in surprise at his story. I hadn't known him long and already what he had just told me seemed out of character.

He nodded. "Yeah, I know. I was hot-headed. Still am, sometimes. But we'd never really gotten along that well. Never saw things eye to eye. You know what I mean?" he asked.

I nodded.

"That was the final straw for both of us though. I walked out and told him he could do whatever he wanted with the place because I wasn't going to be there to watch it go under."

"You quit?"

"Damn straight. We just couldn't work together. I knew it and he knew it."

"So what happened?"

"Well, about a year later, he called me, out of the blue, and said he wanted to talk. I went in to the store not having any clue what he wanted to talk about. I swear it looked just like it did the day I walked out."

"You hadn't been in since?" I asked.

"Nope, not once. Hadn't even seen my old man. I think we were both glad to see each other but neither one of us had what it took to apologize. We were riding two proud horses, that's for sure. Finally, he told me that he wanted me to buy the store. I just laughed. He knew I didn't have any money, and truthfully I figured he was offering it to me as a last resort. I doubted whether he could find anyone else who was even interested. I didn't say that, but that's what I thought."

Danny raised an empty glass to get April's attention. She held up two fingers in question and he nodded.

He continued with his story. "Anyway he had worked up a plan where I would make payments to him from profits. Then if I ever got it paid off I'd pay him a monthly amount for just having made it possible. It sounded pretty good because my job sucked and I hated it. But, I didn't say yes immediately. I could of, I suppose. But I didn't feel like I had any bargaining chips at all. And like I said, I thought it might have been a last-ditch effort on his part."

"So, how long did you leave him wondering?" I asked.

"Not long, a couple weeks maybe. Maybe not even that long. Mom confided to me that it wasn't a last ditch effort. She said he hadn't even approached anyone else, and that it had been his plan all along for me to have the store. Things just didn't follow the path that he had hoped for. Well, that changed everything for me. Like I said, I had known immediately that I wanted to do it. So, after that we made an agreement which included us working together for 90 more days. During that time he would help me with things that I hadn't done before and then I would be on my own. I'm here to tell ya', brother, that was the longest 90 days of my life." Danny laughed loudly and his reaction caused me to join in.

"So you were kind of in the same situation that I am," I offered.

"Yeah kind of, I suppose. But the old man would have been there to answer questions if I got in a bind. There again though, the Millers have always been a prideful bunch. My ego didn't let me ask him for advice. The other side of that is that the business was on the decline with him at the helm anyway, so it wasn't like he was a fountain of insight."

I interrupted him. "I really want to know how you got from there to where you are now. Would you be willing to share any of that with me?"

He laughed and said, "Hell yes, if you're buying, I'm sharing. I'll story all night," he said.

"You got it," I replied. "Small price to pay for a good story."

"You'll think small price when you watch me chow down on the largest steak they can dig up at the Beach."

***

We ordered dinner. Danny wasn't kidding about the steak! It was huge, but man was it worth the investment. I sat and listened to him like a disciple to a guru.

"So," I said, "if I shouldn't concentrate on cutting expenses, what, then?"

"That's easy, Charlie. Even I knew that when I took over." Twinkling eyed, he paused for a moment and then added, "that's about all I knew, but I was aware that we had to increase top-line sales. Early on I was lucky to meet a couple guys who helped me figure out how to do that."

"Who?" I asked.

His smiled sheepishly and then said, "Maybe I'll tell you ...

eventually. That is if you buy me dinner enough times."

We laughed together again and I had the feeling that we were going to be friends for a long time. I also knew he wasn't going to tell me about the mystery men, at least not yet. Have you ever met a person with whom you felt an instant connection? Well that's the way I felt about Danny, and he's told me more than once that he felt the same way about me that first night at the Beach House.

I restarted the conversation, "But I told you about the competition and all. How do I control that?"

"Son, you've got to control the things you can control and forget about the rest," he said very stoically.

He appeared to be only 10 or 12 years older than I was, so I had no idea where the "son" thing came from, but actually I didn't mind.

"Can you stop the big box from being there?" he asked, "Or the Internet from Internetting or whatever the heck it does? Can you control the economy or the weather?" He paused, just momentarily. "No? Well then, why in the world are you fixating on those things? *Change the things you can control.* There are plenty enough of those things to allow you to fix your problems."

"You really think so?" I asked.

"I do," he said, nodding. His demeanor softened. "Listen Charley, I was shootin' straight when I told you that I've been where you are now. You know what? I used to look at my store, and then I'd look at others around here, and stores in other areas, too. And in every market there were stores like mine, you know—the ones that were clearly struggling. But then there were the others, the ones that I wanted to imitate; they were like *Stores on Fire*. You know, they were just killing it. I wanted my store to be one of those. So, I set out to learn how to manage better. And, I'm going to brag a little, I've done pretty well."

"Help me Danny; give me some clues about what you've

learned and where I should start."

"I will. It's going to be a learning process, but if you're willing to learn, I'm willing to share."

I most assuredly was.

***

"I guess you look at your P&L every month, right?" he asked.

"Yeah, unfortunately I do," I said, thinking myself funny.

"The top part has all your sales listed. Cash and charge, right?"

"Yeah."

"What comes next?" he asked.

"What comes next?" I puzzled.

"Yeah, what's the next section on the Profit and Loss report?"

"Cost of Goods, I guess."

"Yep, and what happens when you subtract the cost of goods from the sales?

"What happens? I'm not sure I understand," I said.

"You get your gross profit for the month. The cost of goods subtracted from the month's sales gives you the gross profit number." He paused.

I felt like saying "well duh," but it was too early in the relationship for that.

"That's simple enough, right?" he asked.

"I guess," I said. "It's simple, but I don't know where you're headed."

"This is where I'm headed. You need to raise your store's *baseline performance*. If you do that, you'll have a higher launch point each month."

"Forgive me, Danny, I'm lost already. I don't even know what you mean by baseline performance." I moved my head back and forth, somewhat exasperated that I didn't understand what he was saying.

"Ok, here's what I mean," he said as he took a blank napkin from the holder and began to sketch. "Let's say we build two rockets."

"Oh, no," I said, rolling my eyes. "It *is* rocket science."

He smiled, pretty much ignored my comment, and continued to draw. "These two rockets are identical in every way." He continued, "They're made of the same material and weigh exactly the same amount. So we haul them to a desert where the elevation is zero. It's sea level. You still with me?"

I nodded.

"OK, we take the first rocket and we do a count down. Five, four, three, two, one and we push the launch button. We hear it roar and see it leave the ground. It leaves a vapor trail and goes up into the sky a long way. But then it runs out of gas, fuel or propellant or whatever made it purr. Anyway, it stops climbing. Somehow we're going to magically suspend gravity for a while and it's going to just dangle there at the highest point of its flight. Can you see it?"

I acknowledged that I could. I loved his passion. He was a natural born story teller.

"Ok, now we're going to build a tower. We're going to make it 500 feet tall. Next we hoist our other rocket up there. We take great pains to fill it with exactly the same amount of fuel. We do our count down again and push the button. It takes off. It keeps climbing and we notice it reaches the other rocket and then flies on by." He made a wild gesture with his hand to emphasize the image.

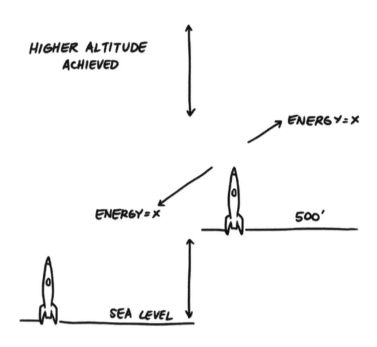

"When it eventually runs out of fuel, gravity is still suspended. Which rocket flew the highest?" He waited.

"Well, I suppose the second one did," I said.

"Yep, now tell me why. Did it require more propellant?"

"No, it didn't need more propellant. It's simple, the launch point was higher. That's the difference."

"That's what I'm talking about." He pointed a finger and gestured emphatically. He then leaned back and postured as if he had just bowled a perfect game.

"I guess there's a correlation between the rockets in your story and my store? I enjoyed the story by the way," I said smiling.

"Just like the rockets you need to raise your baseline, your launch point, your business as usual. And the "as usual" is the key. If you do that, the same amount of effort will take you to higher profits, just like the higher launch point took the second rocket to a higher altitude."

"My 'as usual'?" I asked.

He studied me and then continued to explain. "On any given day, you have an amount of customers come in, "as usual." You have a conversion rate that your store produces "as usual." Your store has an "as usual" transaction size and an "as usual" margin on sales."

"Conversion rate?" I asked.

"Yeah, conversion rate. Say you have 100 people come in and you sell something to 65 of them. Your conversion rate was 65 percent. Or, in other words, you converted 65 percent of your opportunities into paying customers."

"But you can't know the number of people that come into your store, can you?" I asked.

"Sure you can. Install traffic counters on all the doors and you'll know. The ones I installed were not expensive, and the numbers have really been eye opening for me. I thought our conversion rate was much higher than it turned out to be. But with some hard work and good strategies we've improved it, that's for sure."

We exchanged more conversation, but I could tell that Danny was as tired as I was. It had been a long day, but a good one.

"How early you heading out in the morning?" he asked.

"I thought I'd hit the road around seven or so. Why, did you have something else in mind?"

"Well I was going to suggest that you stop by the store in the morning. We have our weekly store meeting at seven. If you'd like to be there, you're welcome. You might find it helpful. And then I'd like to talk more about raising your baseline performance. Are you game for any of that?" he asked.

"Sure, I'll make time. I'll be there at seven."

He reached for the check, but I grabbed it out of his hand. "No way are you paying for this."

The drive back to the store was quick. When we turned into the parking lot, my question about how the store looked at night was answered. It looked awesome! The lighting and identification made the store impossible to miss.

Chapter 4

The phone rang early the next morning. I was already up. I had showered and dressed and was opening the drapes to enjoy the view.

The caller ID showed that it was Julie on the phone.

"You're up early," I said.

"Yes, I was. You were awake too, weren't you?" she asked, almost sounding apologetic.

"Yeah, I've been up for an hour or so."

"How was your night?" she asked.

"It was good. I learned quite a bit. I'll tell you all about it later. But I've got to keep moving right now. I'm going to stop at the store this morning. I have several questions about things Danny covered last night, and he invited me to listen in on their store meeting.

"Store meeting?"

"Yeah, I guess each week he has all his employees gather for a meeting. I'm not sure what they talk about, but I guess I'll find out."

"Do you do that at our store?"

"No, you're dad never did, so I didn't even consider it. Didn't even know about it."

I had purposely mentioned her dad to check to see how she was really doing.

"That should be interesting," she said, ignoring the reference.

"How was your day?" I asked.

"It was good, really good. Charley, I think I'm doing better."

"That's awesome to hear, Julie. I've been pretty worried about you."

"Thanks. I know things have been hard and that I've not been the most pleasant companion for a while ... for quite a while."

"I don't think I have either," I replied. "But I woke up excited. It's funny how just a few hours with this guy has affected me. If I can learn from him and get the store doing better it will ease some of our financial worries, and I think we'll both feel better."

The small talk continued, but I can't tell you how awesome I felt. To notice that she was doing better, and then to have her actually acknowledge it, was the perfect way to begin a day.

***

When I pulled into the lot there were several cars parked along the side. There was a guy washing the front windows. As I walked to the entry I wondered how long it had been since our windows had been washed. I couldn't recall.

"When you finish here, you can come wash the windows at my store," I called out.

The young man stopped what he was doing, smiled, and said, "I might take you up on that if you'll help me deliver some shingles."

"I'll think about it," I said as I pushed the door open.

I entered the store and noticed several people gathered around a service desk down a secondary aisle.

"Hey Charlie, come on back." I saw Danny motioning for me to join the group.

"Hey everyone, this is Charlie Kern. He's a friend of mine. He owns a store kind of like ours up in Missouri. If you see him nosing around, that's ok. He and I are sharing some information. So if he asks you any questions, answer them the best you can, OK?"

Nice, I thought, as I nodded to the group. "Hey everyone."

"OK," Danny said, "let's get started. Barry you have the program, don't you?"

A tall good-looking 20-something kid nodded. "Yep, it's my turn. How's everybody doing?"

A few people responded, some grunted, others just smiled.

"Ok, good job everyone. Our conversion rate for the month was up two and a half percent over last month and almost five percent over a year ago."

"Good job people," bellowed Danny. He started clapping, and one by one the group joined the celebration.

Barry continued. "We had some seasonal mark-downs in Lawn and Garden, so we took a hit on margin last month. But with your efforts on the end caps we minimized the impact. We're still up a little over a point for the year. Danny said he was excited because we're going to hit the goals that were set for bonuses this quarter, and if we do, I mean, when we do" (I heard some hoops and hollers from the group) "that'll be eight quarters in a row. Two full years. Good job everyone."

"Let me see," he said, checking his notes. We have a circular coming out Friday of next week. All of the products are here, the sales support material is in the cage in the receiving room. Joe, you and Tina make sure that it gets up at the appropriate time, and when you do, double check to verify that we have each item. OK?"

I noticed their acknowledgements.

"Everyone else, study the ad, and if you have any questions, get with me or someone else and find out where everything is. Also when you locate the items start thinking in terms of what else the shopper could use with each one or what will make the items work better or the application of the items easier. Commit those things to memory. Share and discuss them among yourselves, and then suggest those add-ons with each customer. Let's drive our transaction size up again."

"One other thing here in my notes. If you haven't completed the training on selling the new window line, make sure you do that before month's end. Remember if you fail to complete your required training modules you forfeit your bonus, and no one wants that to happen." He paused before adding, "I guess that's all I have. Anybody have any other comments, questions, or suggestions?"

A woman raised her hand.

"Yeah, Mary, what's up?"

"A guy came in yesterday and was griping about our prices. I don't know what to say when someone does that. Any suggestions?"

Barry glanced at Danny, but Danny nodded a "you handle it" look, so Barry fielded the question.

"You know, we could give everything in the store away and some people would still complain that we were too high. I know it's uncomfortable, but what we need to focus on is that our store's operating margin is right at national averages for this type of store. That shows me that we're priced about right. Remember, we have to maintain margin in order to pay salaries and the bonuses that we all like. As far as handling the complaints, always listen politely, of course." He thought for a moment and then added, "A good response might be something like 'we feel that our prices represent a good value when you compare quality, convenience and service.' Don't get me wrong. That's not going to satisfy a person who's already upset, but, it shouldn't escalate the situation either. It's probably as good of a way as any to disengage from a no-win conversation." He paused, looked a little apologetic, and then asked, "does that help?"

"A little, maybe," resigned the lady. "But I just hate to hear people say that. That's all."

"Yeah, me too, Mary. I think all of us feel the same way in that regard." said Barry. "But," he shrugged his shoulders, "we're not going to please everyone, even though we'd like to and try to."

Danny interrupted, "Great stuff, you guys, thanks for your hard efforts. I'm proud of our store and particularly this crew. That's you and you and you and you ..." he went on pointing at each individual in the group. "Let's get this joint opened up and sell something."

He turned to me and said, "Come on, Charlie, I'll show you my office."

I followed him to the back.

***

Danny's office was nice, not overdone, but classy and comfortable. I noticed, unlike my desk, his was clear and the work area organized.

"Cup of coffee?" he asked.

"No, thanks, I ate at the motel. I'm good."

"I think I'll grab one. I'll be right back," he said, disappearing into the hallway.

I looked around and noticed that there were no pictures of family on the shelves or desk. It occurred to me that I hadn't even asked.

He returned shortly.

"So, you married, Danny?"

"No, not yet. Maybe one day, but I don't really have the time to go shopping around," he smiled.

"Maybe you need some home delivery," I suggested, and we both chuckled.

"Someday, maybe. We'll see." He tilted his head to the side and shrugged his shoulders.

I took the conversation a different direction. "I have to tell you that I was really impressed with your store meeting and how engaged your employees were. So, you share results with them every month?"

"Yeah, I do. My old man would have never stood for it, but

I don't think I can use performance as an incentive if nobody knows how we're doing. Plus it's just a great teaching opportunity. It allows me to teach and it allows them to learn from me and from each other. And truthfully, I learn from the conversations too. For example, the thing about the price complaint made me realize that it's been a while since we've done a price comparison. I like to do that once a year or at least every other year. After we do it, if we look competitive, which I think we will, we'll share the findings. If we learn that we need to do some adjusting, we'll do it and then we'll share that, too. Either way we win. Either way it demonstrates to the staff that we're doing everything we can to put the store in a good light. And, I'm here to tell you that if your employees think you're priced fairly that comes across in their communication with customers. So that's something we work really hard at."

"And this Barry kid? Is he an assistant manager or something?" I asked.

"No, not currently, but he's a guy that has the potential to manage a store for me some day. He's one that I bring in to the office regularly to discuss strategies. He, and a couple others, I'm grooming them for managerial positions. We discuss plans for the future and ways to raise our baseline."

"Other managerial positions? Do you have other stores?" I asked.

"No. Not yet. But I have a big vision for what we could accomplish one day. And, in order to hire quality people you have to paint a picture of opportunity. So, we're constantly discussing expansion and what that might look like. It keeps them enthused and me, too. In fact, the visions that I use to speak of were just hazy day dreams. But now they're starting to take form. I have a leasing agent doing some preliminary work for me in a town about

40 miles south of here. When I find the right opportunity I'm confident that I have someone ready to go. It's all pretty exciting and it started with just a smoky vision."

"I can only imagine," I said, contrasting his operation against mine.

"Well, imagining is always the first step," he replied.

I took a moment to catalog that comment and then changed the subject again. "Oh, by the way, I want to hear more about raising the baseline. We talked about it last night and you showed me the rocket thing. But I need to understand more about what that all means."

"Last night, when I used the rocket illustration, did you get the analogy?" he asked.

"Yeah, I think so. The platform illustrated a higher launch point for the rocket, much as if we raised, I think you called them our 'as usuals' would raise our store's launch point."

"That's it," he exclaimed.

"Ok, I get that. But tell me more about the 'as usuals' and how you leverage that knowledge. That's the part I don't get."

"I told you that your store has an 'as usual' amount of selling opportunities each day."

"Customer count, right?" I asked.

"Yep, that's right. And it has an 'as usual' conversion rate. Remember that?"

I nodded.

"Beyond that your store has an 'as usual' average transaction amount and an 'as usual' margin that it produces. Follow me?"

"I guess, but those numbers vary from day to day certainly, and week to week, too."

"You're right. Nothing is constant. But looking at the big picture, over time, those numbers comprise your 'as usuals'."

"So, when you say 'as usuals' are you just talking about averages?" I asked.

"Yes and no. If you think of it as averages you start thinking in terms of longer periods. Also, it's post-event measurement, as in 'what did we average last month?' The reason it's so powerful to think of daily and weekly 'as usuals' is that you begin to understand that you don't need to make big improvements to make huge differences. And it also allows you to actively change procedures to produce better results before the measurements. Then, averages, when they're measured, assess the results of your actions."

I shrugged and said, "Seems like splitting hairs."

"Maybe, but for me it's very empowering. For example, I know our customer count is around 200 people per day. That gives us 200 selling opportunities. Some days are less and some days are more. But when we strategize, we think in terms of how we can increase our customer count by two or three people a day ... this day. We don't focus on averages. When you think of increasing traffic by two or three a day, it's easy to conceptualize," he said.

I nodded in agreement. "I see that." I paused momentarily before adding, "but two or three more people a day doesn't make the kind of changes I need. And to think in terms of a 73 percent conversion rate instead of 69 percent or a 26 percent versus a 27 percent margin wouldn't help that much, either. I need something bigger."

"You think so?" he asked, smiling. He opened his desk drawer, fumbled for a moment and then pushed a yellow writing tablet my way. "Here's a pad and a pen. I think you're going to want to write this down. Do you remember when we talked about top-line gross margin dollars and how it was derived from a simple equation? You know, sales minus cost of goods?"

"Yes, we were talking about the P&L, and that's where the conversation went."

"I want to show you something that I learned that's called the Opportunity Equation. It shines more light on how that number is actually produced. It's not as simple as the P&L leads you to believe. In fact, it's kind of a hidden equation." He began to draw a chart. "OK, we start right here with our number of selling opportunities, our customer count. That number multiplied by conversion rate results in transaction count. You with me so far?"

I nodded, smiled and said, "I suppose you learned this from the mystery men, too?"

He ignored my comment and continued, "OK, the transaction count times the average transaction size gives us sales for the period, whatever period we're examining." He looked to affirm that we were still together and this time I nodded silently.

"Multiply that number by margin and you'll see that it results in the same figure as subtracting cost of goods from total sales .... the top-line gross margin dollars. The difference is that now we've isolated four variables that we can focus on to help us improve our results."

I thought for a moment and then said, "That's where you were trying to take me when you mentioned the 'as usuals,' they were customer count, conversion rate, transaction size and margin."

"Bingo."

***

"So, what's your average transaction size?" Danny asked.

"We sell some bigger tickets. I'm guessing it's around $60, but I'd have to check to make sure, it may not be that high."

"And your margin?"

"27, maybe closer to 28."

"If you had a strategy to improve that, do you think that you could raise it by a point or two?"

"Yeah, Danny, I suppose I could. But you're missing my point. I need substantial improvements, and these small tweaks would be great if I were fine tuning, but I'm not."

"Come around here, I want to show you something." He started slapping some keys on the computer, but continued to talk. "I think this will surprise you."

He opened his browser's "favorites file" and clicked on a link. Once there, he searched around and opened a page showing a calculator titled "The Amazing Results of Incremental Increase."

"Let's fill this in together. Since we don't really know your customer count we're going to use 125 for our experiment, OK?"

"Yeah, I'm ashamed to say I don't really have a clue, so that's fine," I said.

He nodded and then replied. "OK, let's talk about conversion rate. When I first started tracking mine it was about 63%, so we'll use that number for a starting point."

I watched the screen closely.

"Now, I'll enter your $60 average transaction size and I think you said 27-28 percent margin, right?"

"Yeah, that's a guess."

"Ok, I'm going to use 27 percent. And we'll say you're open six days a week?"

"Actually, only five and half. I've thought about opening all day Saturday and maybe even on Sunday, too, but I haven't done anything about it yet."

"We'll use six days. That's fine. I just want to show you

how the thing works anyway," he said, dismissing my comment.

"He pointed to the screen. OK, if these numbers were all correct, you're current gross margin, or top-line profit, would be about $398,000 per year." He grabbed a pen, did some numbers scribbling and then said, "That would put your total sales at about a million and a half. Is that in the ball park?"

I shook my head. "No, they're more than that, but keep going; I want to see how this thing works."

"Ok, sure. We'll get your real numbers when we can, but this will let you see how powerful small improvements can be.

He pointed at the screen again, "If you had a strategy, would it be possible to generate three or four more store visits a day?"

"You mean new customers?" I asked.

"No, three or four more store visits. You have two ways to increase your customer count. You can bring new people in or you can cause your established customers to come in more frequently, or a combination of both. Make sense?"

"Yeah, completely. With a strategy, I think we could do better than that, but three or four should be easy enough," I said.

"OK then, in this cell," he pointed to a blue square on the screen, "I'm going to enter a '4.' so eventually we'll need a strategy that results in four more store visits per day."

I nodded.

"This cell, the one on the right," he pointed again, "keeps a running total of how we're impacting gross profit dollars."

"You mean just that one improvement would produce that big of difference?" I asked in disbelief.

He smiled, nodded and said, "Yep. Kind of exciting isn't it?"

He definitely had my attention now.

He continued, "As I said, when we started measuring conversion rate here at our store, it was about 63 percent. We were able to increase it by 5 percent rather quickly. So let's use 63 for our starting number, too. We'll enter a five in the improvement cell to plan on a 5 percent increase. So, instead of selling 63 of each 100 customers who come in, our initial goal is to sell to 68 of them. Don't worry about how we're going to do it. That's for another meeting."

I smiled inside. He was actually taking me under his wing. For whatever reason, this near stranger seemed vested in helping improve my store, and that was exciting.

"Transaction size is our next variable. You said that you thought your average transaction size was around $60. What do you think would be a reachable number?"

"With a strategy?" I asked, smiling broadly.

He grimaced and nodded, "Yeah, with a strategy."

"How about one dollar? It seems that should be doable. Maybe even easy," I responded.

"Hold on there, Hoss. Let's be a little more conservative and say 60 cents.

My eyes continued to bulge in disbelief as I watched the improvement that these small changes would bring about.

"The last variable we have to work with is margin." He said, "I'm going to make you get a little more aggressive here. You are operating under industry averages, according to NRHA's Cost of Doing Business study, and quite a bit under what we achieve here. So, what do you think?

"Well, our margin has slipped. We use to run around 30. So, what about using an increase of 3 percent to get back there?" I asked.

"30 would be huge improvement, that's for sure, but let's dial it back a bit. Let's use 28 for the goal. I'll enter a one in this cell for a targeted increase of 1 percent, OK?"

I about swallowed my dentures, and I don't even wear

them. "You mean with just these tweaks I could get that kind of improvement?"

I couldn't believe my eyes. The calculations in this scenario indicated that gross margin dollars would increase by nearly $67,000, which would be almost 17 percent improvement. I was shaking with excitement.

Amazing Results of Incremental Improvement										
Average Customer Count Per Day	X	Average Conversion Rate	=	Average Transactions Per Day	X	Average Transactions Size	=	Average Daily Sales	X	Average Margin %
125	X	63.0%	=	78.8	X	60.00	=	$4,725	X	27.00%
Planned Improvement	X	Planned Improvement	=	Average Transactions Per Day	X	Planned Improvement	=	Planned Improvement	X	Average Margin %
4.0		5.0%				0.60				1.00%

Current Gross Margin $$ Per Year	Targeted Gross Margin $$ Per Year	Gross Profit Dollars Improvement	Gross Profit Percentage Improvement
$398,034	$464,391	$66,357	16.7%

Danny told me a few other things, but I was so focused on what I had just learned that I didn't hear much of it. I was kind of in a trance, I guess. But then suddenly I got this burning ache of uncertainty in my gut.

I blurted out, "Ok, this is all well and good. But, how would I even go about beginning to produce those kinds of changes?"

"It requires processes and procedures to evaluate opportunities. From those evaluations you produce strategies."

By now I was mind dead and he recognized it.

"Tell you what," he said, "I need to get to a job site soon and you've got to get back to Springston. Between now and the next time we talk, think about this: what, exactly, do you manage?"

I was instantly confused again. "What do I manage? I manage a home center, or a hardware store and lumber yard."

He laughed, "Here's a clue. What four asset groups

constitute your operation? Don't think about it right now. Let your mind clear, maybe discuss it with your key people. See what they think and then we'll talk next week.

Chapter 5

I had driven about 30 miles when I decided to call Julie and see how she was doing.

The phone rang only twice before she answered.

"How's it going?" I asked.

"It's been a little slow this morning. I had an appointment cancel. You remember Joanne Durkin?"

"Yeah, married to Bob, right?"

"Yes. Anyway, she's been sick and asked if it was too late to cancel her appointment. I said I was Ok with canceling it because I sure didn't want to catch whatever she had. So, I've been doing some cleaning up here at the shop. How you doing? How was the store meeting this morning?" she asked.

"I'm fine. The store meeting was good ... very interesting. Danny freely shares performance information with this staff. He said that he couldn't get any results based on performance if they didn't know how they were doing."

"That makes sense, doesn't it? she asked.

"Yeah, it does. It's just so different from the way we've always done it. Your dad was so closed mouth about everything. There are many things I hadn't even seen until after the acci..." I caught myself. "Until after I took over." I kept talking quickly. "But, on the other hand, the numbers Danny shared aren't exactly financial data or anything like that. They're more like performance matrixes. The employees seemed to understand it all, so I'm thinking about doing something similar."

"That's good, I guess. So, are you still excited about what you learned?" she asked.

"I am, and I definitely need to be excited. I really do. I understand everything we discussed, but I wonder about my ability to put everything in place. It's really great that he's willing to share. That gives us a better shot at making improvements," I said.

"I don't wonder about your abilities at all," she replied. "You're plenty smart enough, and you work hard. If he'll give you a little guidance, I'm sure you can put it all to work just fine."

I felt better.

"When will you be home?" she asked.

I glanced at my watch. "Probably around two or so if I don't stop for lunch."

"Have you called the store to see how things are going?"

"Yeah, I talked to Kevin. Sounds like things are plugging along. He said a guy left some plans for a new home that he wants some prices on. I'll spend the afternoon working on that. He also said he wanted to sit down and visit with me about something. I'm not sure what that's about. And then I've got to spend some time with what Danny asked me to figure out."

"What's that?"

"He said he wants me to think about, and be able to tell him exactly what it is that I manage. I told him that I manage a home center, but he was looking for something else ... asset groups or something like that. The way he said 'groups,' I know he wants me to think about the operation as if it has more than one facet. So anyway, I want to set down with Kevin and share part of what I learned and see what we can come up with."

"Well it does, doesn't it?" she asked.

"It does what?" I puzzled.

"Has more than a single facet," she said. "You manage many things."

"Yeah, I guess so, but I don't know what he's trying to guide me to. I think he's just trying to help me change my way of looking at things, and heaven knows that I can use that."

***

Getting away from the store for several days was a good thing. I was actually anxious to get back to work. I guess the time spent with Danny had really energized me. When I pulled into our store's parking lot I decided to walk through the front door instead of the back, as was my routine.

It was eye opening. The store looked worse than I realized, and it was sobering. It reminded me of the store located near Danny's. I remembered thinking critically about that one. I thought it looked like it could be going out of business soon, and no one had taken the time to tell the owner. Truthfully, my store looked no better. Perhaps it was even worse, or maybe I was being hyper-critical at the moment. But one thing was for sure, we weren't doing a good job of managing the facility.

Managing the facility? Epiphany. News flash! Perhaps facility was one of the asset groups that Danny wanted me to consider. I was going to include it in my notes anyway. And then I thought; I'm responsible for my store's appearance, but I've never really taken much time to think about how it served as an advertisement for our business. I hadn't really managed it as much as I had just allowed it to exist. We had performed some maintenance, but I had never really considered how it looked and what it said to potential customers. It was just there. As I thought more about it I became convinced that it *was* one of the asset groups that Danny wanted me to consider.

As I made my way through our store, I continued comparing it to Danny's, and as I did, ours didn't show well inside, either. I looked around and noticed that mine was darker and less inviting. His store's unique layout had made it look different and engaging. Mine looked like a hundred other hardware operations, kind of boring and well, blah. I had no signs to direct people and nothing to make the sales area interesting and colorful.

Bobby, one of my clerks, interrupted my thoughts. "Hey Mr. Kern, welcome back. How's your mom doing?"

"She's doing fine, Bobby, thanks for asking. You doing OK?" I asked.

"Yes, sir. Everything's good," he said as he smiled broadly.

Bobby Thompson is a good employee. He's friendly and customers seem to like him. I don't expect he'll stick around long. Sharp kids like him never do, I thought.

"Bobby, have you seen Kevin?" I asked.

"Yeah, he was around here a few minutes ago. I think he went back to his office."

"Thanks, oh, and Bobby, how long has it been since we washed the windows on the front of the store?"

***

I knocked on the door frame. Kevin was looking at his computer monitor and seemed startled when he heard my voice.

"I didn't expect you back until tomorrow," he said.

"Oh, really? Well it feels like a long time since I've been here, and I was anxious to get back."

He smiled, asked about my mother, and listened to my response.

After a few moments of chit chat I said, "Hey, what's up? You mentioned that you had something you wanted to visit about."

I didn't like the way his head and eyes moved as he contemplated his answer. He appeared guarded. "Yeah, I do." He hesitated and then dropped a bombshell, "I've put in a couple applications around, and I just wanted you to know in case anyone calls."

I didn't know what to say. Kevin was a good employee, a

great employee ... my best employee. He was here way before me and even before Julie's parents bought the place. He knew a lot, probably more than I did. I hadn't really leveraged his knowledge and abilities very well. I think it all went back to being overly guarded about sharing. I realized at this moment that if I was going to change the place and really make some headway it would be a whole lot easier with Kevin than without him.

"Oh!" I said not even trying to hide my shock. "I didn't know you were unhappy."

"Well, I'm not unhappy, exactly. It's just that I don't know what the future holds for me here, and I'm not getting any younger. I know we're not doing great, and I worry about what I would do if the store suddenly closed."

I faked a chuckle. "If the store closed? Do you know something that I don't?"

"No," he paused briefly and then continued. "I just know that things seem pretty slow, and I imagine that if things don't change, it could happen."

I rubbed my chin, pondered his statement and considered how to proceed with the uncomfortable conversation.

"You're right about things needing to change, and you know what, we're going to change them. You and me and Bobby and the others. We're going to start planning ways to make things better." I didn't know where my sudden bravado came from, but it felt good to say something positive and hopeful.

I observed a brief small smile on Kevin and noticed that his brow had relaxed a bit. I wondered if he thought my words were simply BS. I continued my silence to let my words sink in and to study his reaction. I wondered if he had already found a job and was just trying to ease his message by revealing the truth a little bit at a time.

"How would we do that?" he finally asked.

"Improve the joint?" I asked.

He nodded.

"While I was gone I met this guy named Danny, Danny Miller. He owns a Home Center down in Freemont, Arkansas. I stopped and got acquainted with him. He has a beautiful and very successful store down there. Really nice guy, anyway ..." I continued and told him the whole story. Retelling the events got me even more excited, and somehow Kevin seemed to pick up on it.

"Four things you manage?" he asked.

"Yes. Four asset groups is how he said it." I watched his wheels turn. He seemed very engaged as I continued. "And I think one of them might be facility, the showroom and maybe even all of the buildings. That would be an asset group, I guess."

He nodded and then asked, "You think another one might be products, or inventory, or whatever you want to call the stuff we sell?"

I thought for moment. "Makes sense to me. It's definitely an asset that we manage."

Kevin seemed pleased. I had a sense at that moment that he was probably shooting straight with me; he had applied for other jobs but had not been offered one yet.

"Ok," I said, "I've got to get to work on that lumber take-off for the Jensen house, but we've got to keep thinking about this because Danny and I are supposed to talk Monday or Tuesday, and then I have to tell him what we've figured out."

"Sounds good."

Chapter 6

"Where did he apply?" Julie asked.

I could see the concern in her eyes.

"Didn't say. Just said he'd put in 'a couple' of applications." I shrugged my shoulders.

"You didn't ask him?"

"No, I was as shocked as you are. And I guess it doesn't really matter where."

"Maybe not, but you need to fix it. He's good help and we depend on him a lot. He's probably your most important employee."

"Agreed, and there's no *probably* to it. He is. Listen, I'm as concerned as you are, and I'm working on it," I said. I then told her how I told Kevin about Danny and our conversations of the previous couple of days.

"What did he say?" she asked.

"I don't know. He's probably skeptical. He's seen and heard a lot of the same old, same old, through the years. He did come up with a good idea on the asset groups."

"Oh, really? What was that?"

"He suggested that the inventory, all the things we sell were probably one of the things that Danny was looking for … you know, another asset group."

"That makes sense, don't you think?"

"Yeah, and I told him so. It's funny I had thought about it for a day or two and had only come up with the facility. I mention it to him, he shoots from the hip and I think he hit the target. I'm pretty sure that we've got two of the asset groups now," I said. "Facility and inventory."

The phone rang. Julie was closer and answered quickly.

"Hello." Her face showed immediate concern. "Hey, Kevin. How are you?" We both knew that Kevin rarely called our home, so we were both thinking the same thing. "Yeah, he's here. Hang on."

"Hey buddy, how's it going?" I said, bracing myself for the worst.

"Employees!" He shouted.

"What?" I asked.

"Employees! You manage employees. You manage facility, inventory and employees!" I could tell he was excited or, at the very least, pleased with himself.

I thought about it for a moment. "Maybe, but would people be an asset group?"

"I would hope you consider us to be an asset," Kevin retorted.

Judging from his engagement level I felt hopeful that Kevin was more frustrated than dissatisfied.

"Sure I do. I probably get too busy to let you know that, but yeah, you and the others, you're definitely assets, so I guess that would make you an asset group."

I paused and then added, "We're going to go with that for our ideas when I talk to Danny. Good job and keep thinking. He said there were four. And, honestly I don't know how being aware of the four asset groups is going to help, but he assured me it would. So, like I said, keep the gears turning."

Chapter 7

The following week was a busy one. I had to catch up from being gone earlier and we had better than average walk-in traffic. The take-off I had to complete from the blue prints took a while because the house was large and had a complex roof line. I was hoping we could land the job, and I felt optimistic. Meeting Danny, and just the idea of potential improvement, had produced a positive change in me, and I liked it.

Tuesday afternoon Kevin knocked on my door. I told him to come in.

"You're not here to tell me you're quitting, are you?" I smiled, but I was dead serious.

"No," he laughed. "But I did have a call to come for an interview at Atlas Aluminum on Thursday."

My heart sank. I felt a twinge of wanting to strike out, but softened instead. "Do you need off for a couple hours on Thursday then?"

"No, I told them I've changed my mind," he said.

I felt like doing a happy dance, but played it cool. "Really? Why?"

"I don't know. I guess since we've been planning together a little bit, I've kind of enjoyed it. I know the lumber and hardware business better than anything else. In fact, it's about all that I really know, and I love it. And, it wasn't that I wanted to leave anyway." He paused and I could tell he was searching for the right words.

"But?"

He hesitated longer, then shrugged his shoulders and blurted out, "It's just that I was not sure you were committed to making the store work. It didn't really feel like you were. But now that we've talked I feel better about it, and better about my future."

I remembered back to my conversation with Danny and his point about having a "grand plan." I decided to plant a vision seed and see where it went. "I'm glad you've changed your mind. You really are important to me. You're important to my plans for the future, too."

"What plans?" He bit immediately.

"I've been thinking. If we can make this store work better, there's no reason why we couldn't have another one someday. There are lots of great communities within 40 or 50 miles. Who knows? Maybe more than two. We've got to figure this one out first, of course. But if we can pull it off, those stores will need managers or perhaps an all-store supervisor. And I know that will all be a lot easier with your input, your help and your experience." It felt good to say. It felt empowering and somehow, suddenly, it felt possible.

It could be my imagination, probably was, but I think Kevin grew a couple inches during that conversation. When he left my office I could tell he was stoked. The thing that I didn't expect was that I felt excited, too. How just visualizing a brighter future could cause my feelings and my attitude to soar, I didn't know.

***

The next couple days with Julie I discovered something that had eluded me. The problems that I had somehow cast as all belonging to her, didn't. When I entered the house that night, she asked me what I wanted for dinner.

"We're going out," I said.

She raised her eyebrows and asked, "Who are you and what have you done with my husband?"

It was cliché and somewhat predictable, but still it made me chuckle. "Come on, it'll be fun."

"Sounds like you've had a good day," she offered.

"I did. I'll tell you about it over dinner. Maybe we can see a movie, too. How about it?"

My cell phone rang. Caller ID showed it was Danny.

"Hey Danny, how's it going?"

"Great, brother, how about you?"

"Better, I think. Hope is a good thing."

He chuckled, "I'll be anxious to hear about that. Hey what I called for is this: Thursday evening I've got to make a trip up to the Bluffs. That's not too far from you, is it?"

"It's about 120 miles or so. Not bad. What were you thinking?" I asked.

"I was wondering if you'd want to meet me for dinner and a couple drinks?"

"Man I would love that," I said, "I think we have the asset groups figured out. I want to see if we're right and see what that gets us."

He began imitating a carnival barker, "You can have your choice of the stuffed animals on the top row." He laughed heartily, obviously amused at himself. "Just kidding. That's awesome. We'll move to the next step if you're right, but you'll keep thinking if you're wrong. Deal?"

"I guess, but I've been thinking about as hard as I can. I've had my key employee helping me, too."

"Oh, that's good. I'm glad you're including somebody. You can't do it alone," he said.

"Yeah, I'm beginning to see that. Hey, would you mind if I bring him along, his name is Kevin?"

"No, not at all, that'd be fine. It might help you keep moving forward. How about 7:00, and are you familiar with place called Pancho's out on 61?" he asked.

"Perfect. I love Mexican food, and they've got great atmosphere there too I've heard."

"Ok, we'll see you then. I'll be looking forward to meeting Kevin. Talk to you later."

After I hung up. Julie was smiling. "Wow, you seem like a different person since you met this guy. I think I want to meet him."

"You mean you want to go with us? You're sure welcome to," I said.

"No. Not this time. I want you to continue to learn from him. I just meant that when someone brings about as positive of change as I've seen in you, I want to meet the guy someday. That's all." She smiled.

"You got it. Come on let's go. Let's get some of that Chinese food you like so well, and I think the new Tom Cruise movie started yesterday".

***

The following morning I was surprised to see that Kevin had beaten me to work. It rarely happened unless I was running late. I decided to walk around the side and go through the front doors again.

Kevin saw me immediately. "Hey boss, good morning."

"Hey Kevin, what's up? You're here early this morning," I said.

"I decided to come in before things got going and see if anything else occurred to me about the asset group thing."

"And?" I asked, "Did you come up with anything?"

"The only thing I thought of was maybe equipment. You know, the forklift, the trucks, the tools we use. What do you think?"

"Maybe, and since we don't have anything else we'll go with those four. Employees, facility, inventory and equipment. We'll run them by Danny and see what he says." I chuckled and then added, "He said if we didn't get them right that we had to keep thinking, so I hope we're right. Oh, that reminds me. I'm meeting Danny down at the Bluffs Thursday night. He said he had to be up there and suggested dinner. Would you like to join us?"

"Sure. I mean, I think so. I need to run it past Rhonda to make sure that she doesn't have plans," he said.

"Ok, sure. Well, just let me know between now and then."

"You know what?" He spoke again almost immediately. "Sure I will. If she has plans we'll change them. This is really important to me. It's important to us. What time?"

"We're supposed to meet him at seven, so we'd leave around 4:30 or so. We're going to eat down there at Pancho's."

"Sounds good. I really like that place," he said.

***

Later that day I was going over the notes I had taken when I was with Danny. I saw that I had written down "*store meeting*" and I had underlined it. I paged Kevin.

It took a while, but he eventually made it to the phone. "Yeah, boss. Sorry it took me so long. I was with Cecil Patterson and you know how that can be." We both laughed.

"Yes, I do. Listen, when you get a few minutes, come back to my office, would you? I want to run something by you," I said.

"Let me make sure we're caught up on the sales floor and then I'll be right there, Ok?"

"Sure that's fine. No hurry, take care of business first."

About 15 minutes later he rapped on the frame of my opened door.

"Sit down. Hey listen I don't think I mentioned it, but that morning when I went to Danny's store they were having a store meeting."

"Store meeting?" Kevin asked.

"Yeah, they discussed some goals they had set and talked

about an advertisement they had coming up. They had a brief discussion about a lady who was complaining about their prices."

Kevin laughed and asked, "Was it just one lady and you say it was a brief discussion?"

I was amused, too, but I didn't want the conversation to get sidelined. "Yeah, it was all good stuff. What would you think about us doing something like that?"

He thought for a moment and then said, "I guess we could. But no one here knows anything about any goals. Heck, I don't even know what our goals are or how we're doing for that matter."

"Yeah, that's on me. But we're going to make some changes for the better. You with me?"

"Sure, boss. What do you want me to do?"

"Nothing at the moment, I guess. We'll talk more about it on our way to the Bluffs Thursday evening," I said.

"Sounds good," he said.

Chapter 8

We pulled out of the parking lot at about 4:30 Thursday evening. I had Clifford, the big red truck, all shined up and ready for a road trip. We left Sherry in charge, so I had no worries. Sherry is more than capable. She worked for Julie's parents from the day they purchased the operation. As I left I silently lamented how poorly I had leveraged her abilities, too.

I looked at Kevin and asked, "You ready for this?"

"Yeah, I'm looking forward to meeting Danny. From what you've told me, he sounds like an interesting guy, and I'm really anxious to hear if we're on the right track with the asset groups."

"Me too. Like I told you before, I have no idea where we'll go from there, but it's been interesting to think about. I told you the rocket story that he told me to illustrate the importance of raising baseline performance, didn't I?" I asked.

"Yeah, you did, but I'd like to hear it again. I'm not sure I got it all. Anyway, it would give me a chance to catch up with you guys."

"You can catch up with me, but we'll still be way behind Danny," I chuckled.

I told the whole story again. I think I even remembered things that I had probably forgotten the first time. It was good for me to recount the conversation. I told him about the equation that Danny had called the opportunity equation and how it worked. I realized that because I hadn't been sharing the P&L with Kevin he was at a disadvantage. That was on me, and I silently vowed to fix it.

"Let me ask you something," I said. "Out of 100 customers that come into the store, how many of them do you think buy something?"

"Wow, that's a tough question," he said. "I don't know."

"I know it is, and I'll tell you right off that I don't know either. I'm just looking for your best guess."

"It seems like we sell most of them, but then again I can think of several people who walked out this week without buying anything."

"Why was that, do you think?" I asked.

Kevin shrugged his shoulders, glanced out the window and then back toward me. "Different reasons I guess. Sometimes we don't have what they want. Sometimes they say we're too high, sometimes they say they're just looking. Other times they say they'll be back, and occasionally they do come back in, but I'm sure there are other reasons, too. I don't know." He shrugged again and raised open hands to indicate he was perplexed.

"Ok, I get all of that. But we really need to figure it out and try to improve, so back to my question. On the average, out of every hundred people that come into the store, how many do think buy something?"

He paused again, "Wild guess, I'd say maybe 75. What do you think?"

I had been thinking about it, off and on, since my conversation with Danny. I had even watched the sales floor more closely to try and figure it out. I was convinced of one thing. Too many people left in a day without buying anything, so I said; "I would have agreed with you before I really started paying attention. But since observing things closer, I'm inclined to think that it's even lower."

Kevin thought for a moment and then nodded. "Could be."

"Do you see how that number, the conversion rate Danny called it, is so important?"

"Yeah, I do. The opportunity equation that he taught only has four variables, customer count, conversion rate, average transaction size, and average margin. So with only four variables, each one needs to contribute at a really high level to produce optimum results."

I was surprised again by Kevin. He sounded a little bit like Danny.

We rode silently for several miles before Kevin spoke again. "I got quite a surprise last night," he said.

"A good one, I hope," I replied, smiling.

He laughed. "Time will tell, I guess, but yeah I think so. Rhonda's excited anyway. We're going to have a baby."

"Holy crap," I said, "Are you serious?"

"Serious as a heart attack." We both laughed again.

"That's great news, Kevin. Awesome!"

***

Pancho's restaurant looked just like I remembered it. It was decorated in the traditional bright oranges and greens that I had seen in almost every Mexican restaurant that I'd ever been in. It wasn't brightly lit, but I couldn't help notice that the pictures and decorations had layers of dust on them. Dust, or maybe it was grease, anyway it wasn't appetizing. But then again, no one came there for the presentation or, at least, I hoped not. They came to Pancho's for the food. The place was not packed but it had a descent crowd.

"How many?" asked an attractive hostess with a pleasant smile.

"There will be three of us," I said. "But, our third is running a little late." (Danny had called from the road.)

"OK, booth or table?"

"A booth please, and if you have one in a corner or at least one that's a bit isolated, that would be great."

She grabbed menus and silverware and said, "Follow me."

We did and she led us to a large round circular booth in a

back corner. "What would you like to drink?" she asked.

"A margarita and water for me," I said. "What about you Kevin?"

"Just water please. Maybe some lemon."

"And bring us some cheese dip and chips, too," I said.

"Queso?"

"Yes, please."

She arrived with the drinks in a few minutes. At about the same time I saw Danny walk through the front door. I stood to motion him over. He saw me, waved, and began walking toward us.

"Hey Danny," I said.

"How you doing man?" He had his big smile on. "This must be Kevin." He reached out to shake hands.

"I've been hearing a lot about you, Danny." Kevin had a pretty good smile of his own.

"Don't believe half what you hear." His laugh was hearty and contagious.

We continued small talk until the waitress returned to take Danny's drink order. She asked if we were ready to order, but we told her it would be a few minutes. We wanted to visit for a while.

***

We talked casually for a few minutes. Kevin and Danny hit it off and had to work through the obligatory manly topics, including hunting, fishing and football. I encouraged Kevin to tell Danny about his new incentive for working harder, and he did. Danny acted excited and happy that Kevin was going to be a father. It was nice to watch.

Danny eventually brought the conversation back around to the purpose of our meeting. "So, what did you come up with?"

"You mean for the four asset groups?" I asked.

He nodded.

"Kevin, why don't you tell him? You thought of most of them anyway." I chuckled a bit, but we both knew it was true.

"Oh, yeah, throw me under the bus," he smiled. "Ok, we decided that it's probably facility, equipment, inventory and employees."

"Wow, you're close, damned close," he said, but then continued. "Facility, yes. Equipment kind of falls in there with facility, so no on that one. Inventory and employees, yes and yes." He looked pleased.

"I don't see equipment being included with or the same as facility," I said.

He shrugged. "Well, here's the deal. We talked about the four variables of the opportunity equation, right?"

"Yes," I said, "Customer count, conversion rate, transaction size and margin."

He nodded and asked, "Have you told Kevin all about that?"

Kevin answered for me, "Yep, he told me about the equation and we worked through some numbers together, so I understand it pretty well, I think."

"Good," he said. "So the idea is to raise the baseline on those numbers. You learned about baseline as well?"

Kevin nodded and smiled, "he even told me your rocket story."

"Great. So if we're going to improve the four variables we're going to have to cause it by changing something about the four asset groups. You'll determine your strategy with that knowledge. So back to equipment, forget about it for the time being. You've got three of the asset groups: facility, inventory and employees. I want you to think again, but this time I'll give you a good clue. Two of the asset groups, facility and inventory are tangibles, meaning you can touch them. The other two groups involve people."

Kevin interrupted, "I guess you could touch employees, too."

Danny laughed and said, "Kind of creepy there, little mister, and you'd probably go to jail."

I sent a look to Kevin to let him know I wanted him to stay focused, but it was too late. The train had already left the rails. The two of them were laughing and enjoying the moment. I eventually joined them for the chuckle.

"Anyway, like I was saying, before I was so rudely interrupted," Danny said, glancing at Kevin which started them laughing again.

I just waited this time until Danny noticed that I was ready to get back to business. "Facility and inventory are right," he continued. "Like I said two of the asset groups are people, and you've already got employees."

He paused for just a moment before Kevin blurted, "Customers. It's got to be customers. Two of the asset groups are people, so it has to be customers and employees."

Danny nodded and smiled, obviously pleased. "Ding, ding, ding." The man wins the prize."

"Ok, so the four asset groups you were looking for are facility, inventory, employees and customers. Is that right?" I asked.

"Yep, that's right. So if you improve any of, or a combination of, the four variables of the Incremental Improvement Equation you'll have to do it by changing something about one or a combination of the four asset groups. Does that make sense to you?" Danny asked.

Kevin was nodding vigorously.

I spoke again. "Ok, clear this up for me. Is there significance to the fact that there are four variables of the opportunity equation, as well as four asset groups?"

Kevin replied before Danny could. "Nope, that's strictly coincidence. He's just saying that to affect the equation, there are a limited number of places to look."

Danny nodded and I felt like I'd been left behind a little. In that moment, I observed how fast Kevin was catching on to things, and I realized that I definitely had to get him more involved. He was even sharper than I had realized.

Danny spoke, "He's right, it's strictly coincidence, so don't get snagged on that."

"You guys ready to order?" the waitress asked.

We looked at each other, nodded, and placed our orders.

***

Our food arrived quickly, still sizzling from the grill. Conversation slowed as we enjoyed our meals. Kevin was the first one finished. He pushed his plate forward and the waitress picked it up almost immediately. Danny and I finished shortly after. The place had lots of empty tables by this time even though it was nearly two hours before closing. We were able to comfortably continue our discussion without fear of disrupting their business.

"Another margarita for either of you two gentlemen?" the waitress asked.

"None for me," I said.

"Me either," Danny said, shaking his head. "But I would have a cup o' Joe."

"Joe?" She asked.

"Coffee, darlin', coffee."

"That sounds good to me, too," I said.

"Cream or sugar?"

"Black for me."

"Same here."

She turned to Kevin, "How about you?"

"No, I'm good," he said.

"How would you like the check split tonight?" she asked.

I held up my index finger and said, "One. Over here."

After she walked away, Danny grabbed a napkin and began to sketch like he'd done the night at the Beach House. "Ok, so here's what we've got." He drew a circle in the center and placed a label inside that read "Increase Top Line." He drew four smaller circles and placed them equally spaced around but slightly overlapping the larger inner circle. "OK, these orbs or circles or whatever you want to call 'em represent the opportunity equation's variables, and the labels on them will describe what you need to do to raise your baseline." He neatly labeled each one in turn, Increase customer count, Increase conversion rate, Increase transaction size, and Increase margin. Kevin and I were locked on his doodling.

He noticed we were very engaged and reiterated, "Ok, the middle circle represents our goal and the smaller ones what we have to focus on to reach it."

Kevin and I were both nodding as we watched. So far, it wasn't difficult to understand. He then drew four other circles about the same size as the first one. Two were placed above the opportunity equation circle and two below. The original circle was now located in the middle of the other four.

"Do the four circles on the outside represent the four asset groups?" Kevin asked. (Just so you'll know that I'm not completely dense, I recognized that they probably did, too.)

"You got it, chief," Danny answered as he finished putting their labels in place. We watched him write, Employees, Products, Facility and Customers on the circles' centers.

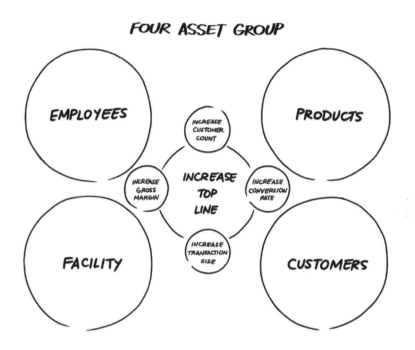

FOUR ASSET GROUP

EMPLOYEES

PRODUCTS

FACILITY

CUSTOMERS

INCREASE CUSTOMER COUNT

INCREASE GROSS MARGIN

INCREASE TOP LINE

INCREASE CONVERSION RATE

INCREASE TRANSACTION SIZE

"OK, study what I've just drawn and think about our conversation so far. We've got the Opportunity Equation goal in the center. Improving the product or the sum, or the answer of that equation consisting of four variables is our path to increasing top line gross margin dollars. Still with me?" he asked.

Kevin nodded and I said, "Yeah, I think I've understood that for a while. I saw in your office last week how powerful the concept is, but where does it go from here? How does it guide our actions?"

He picked up the napkin and tore it into several pieces. At first I thought that maybe I had offended him, although I didn't know why. But quickly I saw that he had simply torn off the four surrounding circles. He set all of them aside except the one labeled "products." He set it picture side up in front of us. He paused and I thought for a moment he was showboating. But, eventually I understood that he was just trying to choose the exact words to communicate the idea.

He finally spoke. "Each one of the asset groups, and keep in mind we're just looking at the product group right now, has a constant cycling process. The fact that the processes are ongoing and repeating is a powerful concept. If we improve any of the steps of the cycle, we leverage those improvements over and over because of the way they keep repeating. Do I have you confused yet?"

Kevin and I looked at each other. I could tell we both were a little cloudy on the concept.

"OK." He said, "That's why I tore this asset group off. We're going to think about it together."

Kevin and I nodded.

"Thinking of the asset group, 'Products' as a cycle, what is the first step of that cycle?" he asked and then waited.

"I guess it would be buying them, buying the products," Kevin said.

"Perfect!" he exclaimed as he drew a small orb at the top of the Products circle. He then labeled it "1. Buy them."

He continued to place orbs around the edge, overlapping the bigger circle. He finished when he had a total of seven.

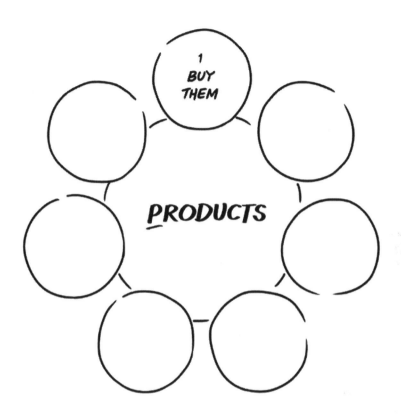

"There may be more steps to this cycle depending on how you do things at your store, but for ours we were able to identify seven distinct steps in our 'Products' cycle. What would you think the next process of this cycle would be?" He clearly wanted to teach us to fish instead of furnishing us with fillets.

Danny repeated his question, "Think about it, what do you think the next step in the Products asset group cycle would be? You've purchased the product, now what?"

"Price it, maybe?" Kevin offered.

"Something else happens before you even have the merchandise in your store," Danny countered.

"I guess you unload it and receive it?" I said.

"There you go. You have the physical processes involved in receiving the product." Danny said, "You unload it, go through a procedure for check in (if you do so) and then you have the physical transportation of the stuff to the sales floor."

Kevin answered first. "Yeah, I guess so, but we price the merchandise in the stock room before we ever move it to the floor."

Danny raised his eyebrows and looked exasperated. "You do what?" And then he quickly continued. "Well then we've found your first opportunity for incremental improvement!"

"What do you mean?" I asked.

"Well maybe I misunderstood you, but it sounded as though you're still physically placing price stickers on each of the items you sell."

"We do," I said.

"Why?" He asked in disbelief.

"Why?" I shrugged my shoulders. "How else would people know the prices?"

He looked away and then back to Kevin and me. "Guys, this is the 21st century. We have these remarkable gadgets called computers and they're here to help us work more effectively and efficiently. A price on a bin label is easily changed when appropriate. When you have to change a price, change it in your computer and change the bin label. Bang. You're updated. The labor hours you'll save by not applying stickers can be put to better use. Actually the same applies to 'checking in' merchandise."

I was confused. "I can see not applying price stickers, but how will we know if we get everything we were charged for if we don't manually check things in?"

Kevin watched closely as Danny answered. "How often do you find shortages? And, remember, I'm talking about your hardware orders here."

I thought about it and knew he had me. "Not very often."

"Can you remember the last time?" he asked.

I squirmed and answered sheepishly. "No, not really."

"And how much have you paid in labor costs to verify that there were no mistakes?"

"Point taken," I said, realizing that if we were occasionally short an item or two we would be still be far ahead money wise by not having to pay labor to check-in and price each item.

Danny continued. "Here's what happened to us when we made that transition. For six months I recorded how many dollars' worth of shortages we found. Turns out it was less than $150. I also recorded how much we spent in labor finding those shortages, and it was nearly $10,000."

I processed what I had just heard. It seemed unbelievable, and yet I had no reason to doubt that what Danny was saying was true.

"But we're getting ahead of ourselves." He continued, "I just want you to think about the rest of the steps of the 'Products' cycle. Did I mention that the steps are called Critical Keys? Anyway, let's fill in the other Critical Keys of the product cycle and we'll call it a night. Then I'll give you an assignment and we'll reconvene later when you've had time to complete it."

***

"OK, let's take another look at the drawing. Remember the products asset group cycle has seven distinct steps. We have filled in the first two; buy them and process them. What do you think would be the third step?"

"I think it must be price them now," Kevin said. He paused to gauge Danny's reaction before continuing. "I mean even if we don't use price stickers we have to consider costs and margin and verify that the price is displayed somehow."

I waited and watched Danny, too. He paused, but shortly his eyes began to twinkle and he nodded affirmation. "Ok, I'll write 'Price Them' in the third process orb."

Kevin was really into the whole strategic thinking process. "I think that the next thing that happens is that the products are delivered to the sales floor and merchandised there," he said.

Danny wrote "Display them" in the next orb as he said, "We kind of have an overlap with hauling the merchandise to the sales floor because it could be argued that transporting product to the floor is part of the receiving process. But when you say the product must be merchandised you're exactly right. It may just be replenishment or it may involve a whole relay of a section. Either way there will be opportunities for improvements that we'll identify as we move further into the process. But back to reoccurring processes ... what are other steps involving products that happen over and over?"

Kevin and I stared at each other blankly.

"Come on guys, we've got five of the eight. Bear down and let's get this done," Danny admonished.

"How about sell them?" I asked. "There are sales processes involved."

Danny nodded silently and then labeled the middle of the remaining three orbs "Sell Them." He then looked back expectantly at Kevin and me.

I spoke directly to Kevin. "Ok, he put 'Sell Them' in the middle. So apparently there's one thing that happens before and one thing that occurs after."

Kevin nodded and said, "The only thing I can think of is that we have to watch and guard against shoplifting. Could that be it?"

Danny began to write again, this time in the orb between

"Sell them" and "Display them." "Yes, kind of. We're going to label this step 'Protect Them.' You're right we have to guard against shop lifting like you said. But we also have to guard against depreciation of product asset values from other reasons, too. Think things like obsolescence, package changes, mark downs, sun fading, damages and all of those kinds of things."

I smiled at Kevin and said, "Ok, we've got it down to the last one. Do you have any ideas?"

Kevin repositioned himself as if he were avoiding discomfort. "Not really. We've gone through the sales process. I guess some kind of follow up might be appropriate with big-ticket items, but for most of the stuff we sell that wouldn't be necessary, so I don't really have any ideas, do you?"

I shook my head as I continued to ponder.

Danny interrupted. "I'm going to bail you out here. This one doesn't happen every time the cycle runs. In fact, we hope it doesn't happen very often, but it is something we have to deal with as retailers."

I raised my eyebrows, shrugged my shoulders and moved my head back and forth. Kevin answered tentatively, "Does it have something to do with closing out things that don't sell?"

Danny's eyes sparkled. "That's it, you got it." He wrote "Purge Them" in the final orb.

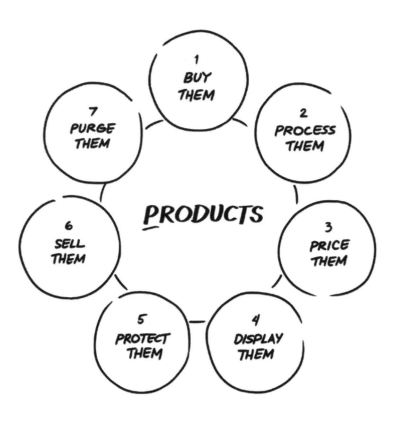

***

"Ok, guys," Danny said, pointing to the Products Asset Cycle chart. "Visualize these orbs rotating counter-clockwise around the "Products" core. The rotation speed varies, but generally speaking the faster the rotation, the better. This process is happening over and over, so any change that results in profit enhancement or labor efficiencies within any of these *critical keys* is compounded every time the process cycles. Does that make sense? It's kind of like compound interest ... it just keeps going."

"I get the concept," I said. "In fact, it makes perfect sense. But, I'm anxious to see how the concept evolves from theory to actionable steps."

Kevin nodded in agreement.

Danny smiled broadly and responded, "That's for a future lesson. But between now and then, I want you guys to go through the same process we've completed with "Products" for each of the other three asset groups." He paused and then added. "Can you do that?"

"Can we do it?" Kevin asked. "Does a bear ship in the woods?"

Danny chuckled and said, "Ship in the woods?"

Kevin said, "Yeah ... like UPS. Does a bear ship in the woods. You know, 'what can brown do for you?'" They both exploded in laughter.

Stores on Fire

Chapter 9

"That was fun." Kevin said as he latched his seat belt.

"Yeah, it was pretty enjoyable alright, but did we learn anything?" I asked.

"I think we learned a lot." He said, "We learned that there are seven, maybe more, but we'll say seven 'critical keys' in the products process. We learned that those critical keys are constantly cycling, and that if we improve anything about them, either in processes or efficiencies, we make improvements to profit. And then, what is really cool, is that because they constantly cycle, when we improve them once we leverage the improvements over and over. To me that's a lot. I can't wait to go through the thinking process with the other asset groups."

I could tell he was genuinely excited.

"Yeah, me too. We need to get on it quickly," I said. "Let's see, tomorrow's Friday. We have a couple big deliveries going out. I doubt that we can work it in then, but how about Monday?"

"Yeah, you're right, tomorrow is toast. Jenkin's Construction is starting the Farley house. We have to take out a load of framing lumber first thing, so I told them to get it staged today. But that'll mean we'll be a hand short out in the yard for a while. So, Bobby will go out to help in the yard for most of the morning. Monday will be better for sure, and that'll give us the weekend to clear our minds and do some thinking about the other asset groups."

"Which one shall we tackle next?" I asked.

"I don't know that it matters, does it?"

"Maybe not, but let's move over to people and work on the Employees group." I suggested.

He nodded and said, "Sure."

We rode on in silence for several miles. I turned on the radio, cranked some tunes and reflected on the evening. I was amazed at Kevin and how involved and engaged he had become. I came to the conclusion that if there was a way to keep him, I needed him by my side as I pushed forward.

"Kevin," I said, turning down the radio volume.

"Yeah, boss."

"You've never had a title with the company, have you?"

He chuckled, "Oh, I've been called a few things through the years. None of them exactly titles."

"I'd like for you to become my assistant manager."

He was quiet. I could tell his wheels were turning.

"Yes, if you're wondering, the title comes with a raise," I said. "We'll start with an extra $100 a week, and when we get things going better we'll revisit it. How's that sound?"

He was now smiling broadly. "I really appreciate it. I needed a raise but I knew you were looking for ways to trim payroll."

"Yeah, I was. But what I'm doing here is something the old-timers call 'betting on the come,'" I said.

"What's that mean?"

"I told you the other day that I was optimistic that we could get the place energized and start producing better profits. I'm now so convinced of that, after working with you and Danny tonight, that I'm 'betting on the come' ... betting on what the future holds."

"That's awesome, boss. I appreciate it and I'm excited."

***

The light was off in the bedroom and I intended to keep it that way so Julie wouldn't be disturbed. It didn't work.

"How'd it go?" she asked.

"I tried not to wake you," I said.

She formed a big sleepy smile and answered. "It's OK. I'm anxious to hear about your meeting."

A few minutes later I climbed into bed.

"It was alright," I said, and then after thinking about the words I had chosen, I corrected myself, "No, it was good. It was really good. It was fun to hang out with Danny again. He's trying to teach us some really incredible stuff."

"Did Kevin enjoy meeting Danny?"

"Yeah, he did, and he was great. He really caught on quickly to what Danny was trying to teach. I was impressed. So much so, in fact, that on the way home, I asked him to become my assistant manager." I paused for a moment and then added. "And, I gave him a raise."

"You did what?" she asked, obviously shocked. I read concern on her face.

"Yeah, I'm tired of not seeing a brighter future, and I want him to be part of it." She didn't answer immediately so I added, "Julie, I really think we can do it."

She smiled, "That's awesome and I know you can!"

We were silent for a few moments. I was just beginning to doze when Julie said excitedly. "Guess what I heard at the shop today?"

I knew immediately what she was going to tell me.

"OK." I paused as if I were thinking about all the possibilities. "My guess is that you heard that Kevin and Rhonda are going to have a baby."

"Oh darn it. You knew already? When did he tell?" She posed as if she were pouting.

"Just tonight on the way down to the Bluffs."

"Is that the reason you gave him the promotion and the raise?"

I thought about it a second, shook my head and said, "It may have entered into my decision. But no, at least, it wasn't the only reason. It was a gut shot the other day when he told me he was looking for a different job. He's a good employee and he can be a key player in what I'm trying to do. I wanted him to know that."

She waited and considered what I had said. "I really do, you know?"

"You do what?"

"I think you can figure it out and get the store going better. You're a smart guy. You may have been lacking experience and direction, but it seems that Danny has already helped some with that. It was a lucky day when you stopped to meet him."

I nodded. "Yeah. It was. I could have stopped at a thousand other places and nothing would have ever come from it. Listen though, we need to get to sleep. It's late."

"Ok," she said as she rolled over, perched on her elbow, and bent to kiss me. "I love you."

"Love you too. See you in the morning."

Chapter 10

The following Monday started off pretty normally. Back then we were only open until noon on Saturday, but it hadn't been my weekend to work. Kevin had left a note bringing me up to speed on a couple things that had happened. Nothing much out of the ordinary, and it looked like sales were just OK. He did say that we were getting a chance to bid a house with a contractor that we had been courting over the last few months. I could tell from the words he chose that he was excited about that. Of course I was, too. He also said that he wanted to meet with me when he came in. Normally, the one who opens on Saturday morning comes in around noon on Monday. I have no idea when or why that started, it's just the way things have always been done around here. I was surprised when I looked up from the papers that were strewn on my desk and saw him standing at the door.

"Hey, boss."

"You're here early. No problems, I hope."

"No, I just thought you might want to get a head start on our asset groups discussion," he said.

I nodded and said, "I have to finish this report for the bank. It'll probably take another 15 minutes or so. You wanna go somewhere and grab a cup of coffee and come back then?"

"I think I'll just hang around if you don't mind. I want to walk the store and do some thinking."

"Sure, no problem," I said. "Think away."

The report I was working on was intended to help assure Fletcher, at the bank, that we were going to be able to meet our obligations for the next six months. Clancy Fletcher, my loan officer, had been overtly supportive since I took over, but he had grown increasingly vigilant over the last few months. I knew it, and he knew it. As I entered the numbers, my mind began to drift. I was visualizing a day when I could go in to the bank and confidently talk to him about the changes we were making. It was going to be a great day, that's for sure. For some reason, my figures didn't come out right the first time. I figured it was because I had been day dreaming. Next pass, no problem. I attached a copy of the report to an email and was ready to hit "send." At the last moment, I decided to go ahead and share a little of the new vision. It couldn't hurt, I thought, so I typed, "Hi Clancy. I have attached the report you requested to this email. Thanks for your continued support. I am anxious to share some exciting things that have been going on around here. We have new focus and resolve, and I think we'll begin to see better results soon. Thanks again, Charley." I reread what I had written, hesitated a moment longer wondering if it was a good thing to let him know what we were thinking and doing. Finally, I decided. I was excited, and I wanted to keep the energy going. What the heck, I thought as I hit send.

I was glad to get that done. It's never pleasant. I'd been sending the reports every four weeks or so. I then responded to a couple more emails, grabbed a cup of coffee and walked out to the sales floor. We were still a few minutes away from time to open, but it looked like everyone was present and accounted for. I found Kevin in the plumbing aisle jotting notes in a spiral notebook.

"So, how's Rhonda doing?" I asked as I walked up.

"She's fine ... planning the nursery. I think things are going to change around our house." He laughed nervously.

For just a moment, my last conversation with Julie about our having children crossed my mind. "Yeah, I bet that's right, but you guys will do fine. I'm sure you'll be great parents."

"Thanks, boss. I appreciate it."

"So, what are you doing?" I asked.

"Oh, I was just making some notes. There are some things I want to get the guys working on. That way when we get started, I won't be interrupted first thing."

"Well, whenever you're ready, come on back and we'll dig in to it. Let's see, where were we going to start?"

"People, I think, specifically employees, is what you said the other night."

"Oh, that's right. Well, anyway, I'm ready whenever you are."

"Ok." He said, "I'll be back in a few."

As I made my way back through the store I began to pay attention to things. Funny, but it seems as if I was suddenly seeing the store through new eyes. I can't explain how or why it happened, but I do know it was kind of shocking. I pulled my phone from my pocket and began taking pictures of departments, end caps, aisles, feature tables, signs, lights and other things. It seemed that I had an awareness that I had never experienced before. I thought the shift might be related to the fact that Kevin and I had been called on to recount small details with Danny on Friday night. When I got back to the office I downloaded the images and put them in a folder on my desktop. I labeled the folder "Before Pictures." I was glancing through them when Kevin came in.

"Sit down," I said. "You get everyone started?"

"Yeah, I think so. I'll go back out pretty soon and check on things."

"Sounds good. Hey, listen, I want to make the announcement about your new title and responsibilities real soon."

He smiled, hesitated and then said, "Well, I think everyone will be OK with it, except maybe Brad."

Brad was, to put it bluntly, a pain in the ass. He was always complaining about this or that regarding the store, and griping about wages and hours. Maybe you know the type. Maybe you've even got one working for you. Anyway, quite frankly, he wasn't good with customers, either. He was short with them, unpleasant and sometimes rude. Honestly, I don't know why I had put up with him except for the fact that he had been there for several years. It felt easier to put up with him than to face the fact that I needed to get rid of him. But, sometimes ruts run deep.

"Well, we'll see," I said. "If he gives you too much grief let me know and I'll handle it, but we'll cross that bridge when we come to it."

***

"Let's get started," I said.

I put a tablet on the center of the desk and drew a circle similar to the one Danny had drawn Thursday night at the restaurant. I wrote <u>E</u>mployees in the center to denote the asset group.

"Does that look about right?" I asked.

Kevin nodded and said, "Yeah, that should work."

"Have you given any thought to what you think the first critical key in this cycle is?"

Kevin reached for his spiral notebook, opened it and said, "Well, as a matter of fact, I have." He smiled. "I think the first step has to be you 'hire them.'"

I considered it for a moment and then answered. "Maybe, I guess. But, it seems to be difficult for us to attract people that could help us raise our game. So, I'm thinking maybe it starts with attracting them. Attracting them, and then I'd go with your 'hiring them' as the second step."

Kevin considered it for a moment and then said, "Yeah, you're right. It's funny. I spent a lot of time thinking about it this weekend, and that never even crossed my mind. But sure, you can't hire them if you never meet them."

As Kevin watched, I filled in the first two *critical key* orbs with "Attract Them" and "Hire Them." I looked up and asked, "What do you have next on your list?"

He glanced at his notebook again and said, "Train them, is what I've got." He waited.

"It's got to be 'train them.'" I said, nodding my head. "Because when you think about it, until the time they are adequately trained and know how to contribute, they're liabilities, not assets. So the quicker we bring them up to speed the better off we are."

Kevin nodded but then interjected, "Yes, but I think where we're missing the boat here, if you don't mind me saying ...

I interrupted him. "You'd better say; you're the assistant manager."

We shared a chuckle before he began again. "Ok, where I think we're missing the boat is that we don't have ongoing training. You know, constant improvement. There's not one of us who wouldn't benefit, and I'm talking about me as much as anybody. You know, product training, skills training, sales training, operations improvement, marketing. Not everything would be appropriate or necessary for everybody, but I think we've got real opportunity for improvement there."

I listened, nodded, and again marveled at how Kevin had gone largely unnoticed to me. I had tried to be an island.

Lost in my reverie, I hesitated before answering, "Ok, I gotcha. I mentioned sitting in on Danny's store meeting, remember?" Kevin nodded and I continued, "That won't do everything that you mentioned, but it would certainly be an easy and inexpensive way to get started. How 'bout you work with everybody and find a time that'll work. Give some thought to what topics you think could help. Remember, we'll keep the meetings short ... no more than say fifteen minutes."

"You want to have the meetings before we open, right?"

"Yeah, most everybody will be here at that time anyway. Try to bring as few people in on their day off as possible. Put a plan together and then let's discuss it."

"And what do you think, once a month?" he asked.

"To tell you the truth, I don't think it would be bad to hold them weekly, certainly, at first anyway. We'll see how they go and how productive we can be with them."

Kevin took notes as we talked. I liked it.

I waited until he finished and then said, "Let's see, where were we?"

***

I glanced at my drawing. "Ok, what do you have next?"

Kevin referred to his spiral notebook again. "Let's see. I don't have a specific order set up, but here are the steps I thought of: schedule them, motivate them, compensate them and supervise them."

"Ok, sorry," I said. "Read them again and I'll jot them down. I guess I wasn't paying close enough attention."

"No problem. I had: schedule them ... motivate them ... compensate them ... and supervise them. And, like I said I'm not sure of the order we'd put them in, but those are the ones I thought of."

I glanced at the note I had just made and thought about the steps he had come up with.

I said, "Wouldn't compensate them and motivate them be the same thing?"

"I considered that at first, but I decided that motivation is not all monetary, you know?"

I nodded as I listened.

He continued, "When you came back the first time from visiting Danny you mentioned that you were impressed by the way his crew seemed to work together. You said they seemed like a really strong team. I thought that sounded cool. If you felt that you were part of a team, you would feel more motivated. It's kind of like the way I feel since we've started working on this improvement plan together. I like the raise you gave me and all, but I have a completely different feeling about what's going on here since I've felt like I was a more important part of it ... like I'm a part of *your* team."

Something in his comment made me feel bad. Why had it taken me so long to consider this? I said, "Ok. You've convinced me. They are definitely different."

I glanced back at my notes. "'Schedule them,' I get. But talk to me about 'Supervise them.'"

He repositioned himself and scooted his chair closer to the desk. "What I was thinking there was after they are trained and have direction, there still has to be open communication systems to make sure expectations are understood and that those expectations are being met. I don't think that part of the process would ever end."

"I thought that's where you were going, but I wanted to make sure. And as far as the process never ending, I think that's the central theme of understanding the *critical keys* of the different cycles. Danny made it clear though that not every step of each cycle would occur when its process occurred. So, in this asset group, the first two steps, Attract them and Hire them wouldn't happen each time. But they're always part of the bigger picture or master cycle."

Kevin nodded. We sat silently for a moment.

"So, do you think we have all of them?" he asked.

I rubbed my temple as I thought. This could make a brain hurt, I thought. "The only other thing that occurs to me is maybe terminate them should be included."

Kevin chuckled.

"No, I'm serious. Every employee, every place in the world has a terminal date. It's a certain occurrence in the employee process."

His smile disappeared as he considered it more seriously. "I guess you're right. It just seemed kind of funny when you first said it."

"Yeah, I know. But I can tell you this. Sometimes you have an employee that you know isn't cutting it. Maybe they just don't have the skills the job requires, or maybe like in our situation here, there is an attitude issue. And you know who I'm talking about. For whatever reason you put up with them, at least I know I have. If I would have had a clearer understanding or a process to address it, maybe I would have taken the steps that I knew were needed."

Kevin considered my words. "Ok, let's put it down. I'm still unclear what Danny is going to have us do with all of these critical keys we're coming up with. We can always take it off our list when he explains the next step of the process."

Chapter 11

Over the next few days Kevin and I continued to hammer out the critical keys of the cycles as we saw them.

We came to the conclusion that there were just five steps in the <u>C</u>ustomers and <u>F</u>acility cycles. This is a picture of the chart we created.

Notice that for facility we came up with: Choose it; accentuate it; present it; heat, cool and light it; and maintain it. The idea is that the last four steps were cycling continuously, albeit slowly. 'Choose it' would just occur if we were relocating, or as my big vision had become by this point, choosing a location for an additional store. Accentuate it, we thought, would refer to how we could make our store more attractive. And when I say more attractive, I'm not talking about just making it prettier. We discussed how Danny's store had attracted my attention the first time I saw it. With his, it *was* pretty. It was very modern and successful looking. Kevin mentioned, though, that he thought a store could attract attention without being brand new or newly remodeled. He mentioned color changes and things like that. And of course, signs on the outside were important. He stated that regarding our store, we weren't great, and I couldn't disagree. We chose 'Present it' to characterize the interior and the stage that we would set for customer experience. The 'heat, cool and light it' is pretty self-explanatory. But truthfully, it wasn't until I had seen how bright Danny's store was that I had given it any thought.

The Customers asset group was harder for us, but we finally agreed on: Identify them, contact them, persuade them, repeat them and collect from them. While we were discussing this one day, a sales rep for a millwork company popped in. I briefly outlined what we were doing and he said, "man, have I got something for you. I'll be right back."

He came back a few minutes later with a small white book in his hand. He said, "I went to a seminar a while back and these guys were talking about some of the things you mentioned. I enjoyed and learned from them so I bought several copies of their book. I'd like you to have one. I think it might really help."

He passed it to me. I glanced at the cover, it was titled, *Discovery-Based Retail*. I told him I thought I had heard of it. I thanked him and although I didn't read it right then, I read it later, and he was right. It did help. It helped us a bunch, in fact. It had a chapter on identifying a store's ideal target customer. That is how we came up with the first step, 'Identify them.'

We thought 'Contact them' was a good way to describe marketing, advertising and an outside sales effort. 'Persuade them' had everything to do with the sales process. 'Repeat them' was basically an acknowledgement that we needed to create repeating customers. With customer count being one of the denominators of the opportunity equation, creating repeating customers seemed critical. We wanted to attract new ones, of course, but it would be their experiences in our store that would keep them coming back. Finally the 'collect from them' might be misleading here. We weren't talking about collecting accounts, although that's important too. For this discussion of improving top-line we were referring to the last stop in the store—the cash wrap experience. I remembered having some bad experiences at checkouts in stores whose names I will not mention. We agreed that cash collection was a constantly repeating process that we could probably improve.

At this point we had all of the *Critical Keys* identified for the four asset groups. We were ready for our next meeting with Danny, although we hadn't set a time or place for it yet. By this time, Kevin had worked out a time and agenda for our first store meeting. He scheduled it for 30 minutes before we opened one Tuesday morning. He told me he didn't think it would go that long, but he felt that the first one would be somewhat unpredictable.

Unfortunately, I didn't get to be there for much of it. Here's what happened. Everyone was standing around the service desk and out into the aisles. Kevin welcomed everybody and explained that we were undergoing some major changes in the way that we were doing things.

At this point I interrupted him. "Sorry to get you off subject, Kevin, but hey everyone, I just want you to know that I have promoted Kevin. He is now the assistant manager. What he says, goes. He's been around for a long time and has functioned more or less in this capacity for some time. I just wanted to make it official and to let you know that he is now your supervisor and no longer just a peer."

Everyone turned abruptly as Brad shouted out, "Well isn't that just fine and dandy. This asshole gets a promotion when some of the rest of us have been here just as long or even longer."

Jaws dropped. To say that everyone was shocked would be an incredible understatement.

I knew I had to react and do so quickly. I stared daggers at Brad and said, "Kevin continue the meeting. Brad, I need to see you in my office."

Luckily, lately I had been thinking about what would happen if I was ever forced into a corner with Brad.

He followed me to the back.

"Shut the door." I instructed. "Brad, we've got a problem."

His face was deadpan, expressionless, as I continued, "I don't know what you think that was all about, but ..."

He tried to interrupt. "I'll tell ..."

I held my hand up in traffic cop fashion and took charge. "Shut up Brad!"

He did as I had commanded, and I continued while he squirmed. "You are no longer an asset to our store in your current position. You won't be working inside anymore. I'm going to move you outside. But even there, I'll have you in a capacity where you're not interacting with the customers."

"Are you done?" he asked.

"For the moment," I responded.

"Ok, now, I'll tell you what. I'm not going to work outside and sweat my ass off all day just so you can make money off of me," he leered.

"You will or you won't work here." I was calm, short and firm.

"You can't fire me like that."

"I'm not firing you. I'm just changing your job responsibilities. Outside is where I have an opening that you can fill, and are qualified to do so."

"Yeah, I'll fill your opening all right. Why don't you stick your job and this place where the sun don't shine? That'll fill your opening." He threw his chair back, hitting and damaging the wall. He turned back toward me at the doorway, gave me indication that I was number one, and stomped out. That was that last time I saw Brad Case. I thought there was a possibility he would contrive a lawsuit or something, but it never happened. Last time I heard he had left town and I really can't say that I was sorry to hear it.

***

"Wow, boss. What the heck did you say to Brad? He stomped out of here dropping 'F' bombs about every other step. He knocked over a floor display in the vestibule on his way out, too."

"On purpose?" I asked.

"I don't know." He shrugged his shoulders, thought about it again and added, "But, nah, I don't think so. He was just pissed off. I don't think he was even seeing straight."

"But he's gone? He left the parking lot?"

"Oh yeah. He left, alright, and he left tire marks and smoke when he did. He could have killed someone the way he was driving. He was really angry."

I shook my head. "Yeah, I know." My heart was still racing from the adrenalin produced by the confrontation.

I told Kevin about the conversation and about the outside position that I had offered Brad.

He looked puzzled and asked. "How would we do that? Who we going to let go out there?"

"Well, if he would have decided to stay, I was going to talk to you about bringing Terrance inside. What would you think about that? I guess we have a spot to fill in here either way," I said, shrugging my shoulders.

He thought about it before he answered. "Yeah that might actually work. He's a sharp kid, and I think everyone would like to see something good happen for him."

"I agree and I believe he's capable. But the main things I like about it are that he's really pleasant and he's good at working with people. He's outgoing and friendly."

"Without Brad in here I think we'll have a more customer friendly environment," Kevin said.

It sickened me to hear Kevin's words and to think about it, but I knew he was right. Why hadn't I acted before? I knew he wasn't good for the store. I can't honestly say, but I imagine it had something to do with me following the path of least resistance. For all that Brad was, there was one thing that he wasn't. He wasn't unreliable. If he was scheduled to open I never had to worry if it would happen. He was rarely sick and I could just count on him being there when he was supposed to be. With my mind focused on other challenges within the operation, I didn't think I needed another one. Funny, though. At this moment I felt a great deal of relief. I knew in my heart that his leaving was a good thing.

"I think so, too. So anyway, think about Terrance coming inside and we'll talk about it again."

"Yeah, I guess we could think and talk about it later, but I'll tell you right now I think it's a good move. He doesn't know much about the things inside the store, but he's been working outside long enough to have a pretty good grasp on things in the yard. I think it would be a good move." He paused for a breath and then asked, "Would we give him a raise?"

I hadn't really considered that yet, but answered spontaneously. "Well, I guess so. It wouldn't be a big one, but I would want him to feel like he was getting a promotion, and I would want him to act like it, too."

"Ok, let me know what you want to do on money and I'll talk to him, or would you prefer to?" Kevin asked.

"No, I want you to do it. I want everyone to know that your promotion was not just lip service. I want them coming to you. I'll take a look at the numbers and decide what we can do. I'll let you know later today, and then you can talk to him whenever you want."

"Sounds good, boss." Kevin said, as he stood up to leave the office.

"Hey, wait a minute, sit back down for a bit. I want to hear how the store meeting went."

He did as I requested and said, "I think it was OK, but just OK. After Brad started yelling when you made the big announcement, concentration was not what it should have been. Then when he stormed out 10 minutes later, cussing like a sailor, I knew I had lost their attention. So, we can't gauge by this one. But we got started, and the next one will definitely be better. I told them to plan on another for next Tuesday. Tuesdays seem to work best, for now anyway."

"OK. Sounds good. Sorry about the circus it created."

He laughed. "Yeah, I didn't even get peanuts."

***

Julie called later that morning to remind me that we had invited Chance and Maria over for a cookout that evening. It's a good thing she did. I had completely forgotten.

"Do I need to pick up anything or do we have everything we need?" I asked.

"Nope, it's all taken care of. I just wanted to make sure you didn't forget and hang around too long after closing."

"OK. Thanks for the heads up. Everything OK at the shop?" I asked.

"Yeah, things are fine. It's been pretty busy. I think business is picking back up."

"That's awesome," I said.

"How about there?"

"Well, it's been an interesting morning, that's for sure. I'll fill you in tonight."

"Good or bad?" she asked.

I laughed. "Depends on perspective, I guess. But good, I think. Like I said, I'll tell you about it tonight."

We said our goodbyes, and as I hung up the phone it occurred to me that Julie was seeming and acting much more like the old Julie ... the one before the accident. This night was huge because we hadn't gotten together with friends for a long time. I was looking forward to it, and even more important, so was she.

Chapter 12

I started the grill at about 6:30 that evening. It was a warm night but it was perfect for a little get-together. Chance and Maria made it over around 7:00, carrying two bottles of wine. After some couples' small talk, we separated. Maria went with Julie to the kitchen. Chance and I could hear them giggling as we grabbed drinks and headed outside. I don't know if it meant anything to him, but for me to hear my wife laughing again ... well, it felt great, like a return to normalcy.

After checking the grill we sat down on the deck and Chance began to tell me about their plans for a Yellowstone vacation that year. He asked if we had anything in mind, and I told him that I thought we'd put it off for a while. I told him that I wanted to stay and continue some work that I had begun at the store.

"Are things going OK?" he asked, and then added, "I mean with the business and all?"

One thing you need to know is that Chance and I have become close. He was always coming over, checking on us after the accident. If we needed help of any kind, he was the one we called. He's a "hands on" kind of guy who runs his own machine shop. So, I didn't mind sharing with him. In fact, I welcomed the opportunity.

"It's been tough, Chance. I didn't have a background in this at all, and Julie's been ... well, you know how Julie's been."

He nodded as I continued, "But things are changing. I met this guy who has, for whatever reason, chosen to help me."

I relayed the story about Danny, how I'd stopped and met him and about our meetings. I told him about promoting Kevin and how much help he had suddenly become.

"That's great," he said. "You sound really excited."

I thought about it for a moment, processed my feelings and answered. "I am. I really am. I feel like I have been treading water, reacting to whatever happened. But Danny has given me a glimpse about what it's like to understand a bigger picture and maybe, for the first time, understand what managing the store might look like. I'm not there yet, but the light at the end of the tunnel may not be a train after all."

Chance laughed and then took a long drink. "I heard what happened today," he said.

"Happened where?"

"At your store. I heard about Brad quitting."

"Wow. That was quick."

He laughed again. "Yeah news travels pretty fast in a town this size."

"Who told you, and what did they say?"

"Larry told me," he said.

"Larry?"

"Larry Dickerson. He's Brad's cousin or nephew or something like that."

"Oh yeah, I know who you're talking about now. Well, what did he say?"

"He told me the whole story ... the story from Brad's perspective anyway."

He laughed again before continuing. "Then he said that he didn't know what the heck took you so long to run him off. He thought Brad had chased away more business than he had ever helped bring in. And I have to say that I agree with him. He was OK with me, but I thought he treated most people pretty rudely. I know a lot of people said that they started going to Builders' Market just because they didn't think your store was very friendly."

"Now, why the hell didn't you tell me this before?" I asked incredulously.

He took another swig and pondered my question before

replying. "Really, Charley? You couldn't see it yourself?"

This time it was me who thought before speaking. "Yeah, I guess I knew it. I just put it off. Didn't want to deal with it."

Chance lightened the moment. "Well, anyway, it's probably better for you and him both. If he wasn't happy, this will give him a chance to find something that he'll like better. Who you gonna replace him with?"

I told him our plan and he agreed that it was good one.

"You know what I think you ought to do?" He asked.

"Tell me."

"I think you ought to put an advertisement in the paper. Have them put pictures of your employees in there and just have them title it "meet our friendly staff" or something like that. People who were off-put by dealing with Brad won't even know he's gone if you don't tell them."

"I guess they wouldn't. Would they? I might do that. Hey, listen, I think those chops should be done. I'll take them up. Let's go eat."

***

"So, he just walked out?" Julie asked, as she rolled over in bed to face me.

"Yep."

"Well I think it's a good idea to bring Terrance inside. I think he'll do great."

"Yeah, me too."

We were silent for a few moments and then I asked, "Did you enjoy the evening with the Binghams tonight?"

"I did. It's been a long time since we've had friends over. Charley ..." She was suddenly hesitant.

"What?"

"I'm sorry I've been the way I have for so long."

I looked into her eyes, put my arm around her, and pulled

her close.

"It's understandable. I know what you've been going through. I'm really glad to see that you've been having a few good days mixed in now and then."

She smiled, snuggled closer and we drifted off to sleep.

Chapter 13

Over the next couple weeks, for whatever reason, things got a little busier. Kevin was flourishing with his new title and responsibilities. He had talked to Terrance about our plan. Terrance, Mr. T as we had begun to call him, was thrilled to be given a promotion and offered new opportunities. He proved quickly that he had been a good choice. He began training himself in product knowledge and was willing to take on any task that was assigned him. As I had suspected, the community was happy for him as were the other employees. We were going to have to replace him in the yard, but we were in no big hurry to do so. Everyone just took on a few more responsibilities and we were making it work.

I was working in the office one day when Sherry popped her head in. "Charley, I'm sorry to bother you but there's a Danny Miller on the phone. I told him you were busy, but he said he thought you'd want to take his call."

"I do, Sherry. Thanks, I'll just take it in here. Close the door on your way out, would you?"

I waited a moment as the door closed and then I picked up the phone.

"Hey, Danny. What's happening?"

"Busy, brother, busy. How about you?"

"Well it feels like things have improved a little."

"Really? Tell me more about that."

I caught him up on things ... Kevin's promotion, Brad's departure, told him all about Terrance and some other small victories.

"Man, that's exciting. Sounds like things are beginning to roll. Tell me, have you had a chance to work on the *Critical Keys* for the other asset groups?"

"Yeah, we've got them done. We finished them a week or

so ago, but with everything else that's been going on, I just haven't gotten around to calling. We're excited to show you what we came up with and to learn what we need to change. But mostly I'm excited to find out what the heck we do with them."

"Cool, brother. That's why I'm calling. I want to come and see your store and help you get on the road to some improvements."

"Wow that sounds awesome. When do you wanna do it? We're all in."

"I was thinking about next weekend if it works for you. I was planning on driving up on Friday evening. I'll get a room and then we can meet for breakfast Saturday morning before you open. Then we'd go to the store and spend however much time you want on it."

"That'd be great. But you're not going to a motel! You're coming to spend the night with us. Julie's been dying to meet you."

He was quiet for a moment. "You sure, brother? I don't wanna put you out."

"Are you serious? Put me out? No. I wouldn't have it any other way. You're going out of your way to help us. I'll buy your gas, pay you for your time and whatever else I can do, too."

"Hold 'er right there mister. You'll do none of that. Ok, I'll stay at your house, but I want to help and I'm not doing it for any other reason."

We made more small talk and solidified plans. I was jazzed.

***

"Hey Kevin. I just got a call from Danny. What does your Saturday look like? You're scheduled to work, aren't you?"

I motioned for him to sit down.

"Yeah, I work that morning, no big plans for the afternoon

though. What are you thinking?"

"Danny is going to be here Friday night sometime. He's going to stay with us and then Saturday morning he's coming down to the store to look it over and to meet with us to talk about the Critical Keys we came up with."

"Cool. I'll probably have to be in and out some with working the floor and all."

"Who else is scheduled?"

"Bobby, Terrance and me inside."

"Why don't you ask Sherry if she'll come in, too. I don't want us to be interrupted if we can help it. Danny's making the trip and we owe him that. Besides, this is really important."

"Gotcha, boss. I'll talk to her when we get done here. I know she'll work unless she has something already planned."

I nodded, opened a desk drawer, pulled out a folder and handed it to him. "Would you take these sketches of the critical keys we made and clean them up some so when we talk to him we'll look organized?"

"Sure, boss. I can do that. I'll do it tonight."

***

I was disappointed to learn after a short conversation with Danny late Friday afternoon that he had to change his plan. He was not going to be able to get out of the store as early as he thought. He was still coming, he said, but he wouldn't arrive in Springston until perhaps as late as midnight. He didn't want to disturb Julie and me at that time of day so he made reservations at a local motel. We met the following morning for breakfast and then he followed me to the yard. We walked through the front doors and back through the store. I noticed he was taking everything in, but didn't say much.

After we made our way to my office I said, "Have a seat, Danny. I'll get Kevin back here. I want him in on this."

"Sounds good. Is that your boat in that picture?" he asked, pointing to the image on my wall.

I laughed. "No, it's a boat in my future."

"Well, you've got good taste. It looks fast."

Kevin walked in, approached Danny and extended his hand. "How you doing, Danny?"

"Fine, brother, you doing ok?" Danny asked. "I hear you've been shaking some things up around here."

"We're trying."

After a little more small talk, I asked Kevin. "Do you have the folder?"

"Yeah boss," he said as he handed it to me.

I took the drawings that Kevin had recreated and placed them on the table. They were upside down for viewing from my side of the desk but upright from Danny's and Kevin's perspectives .

I smiled at Kevin. "Wow, these look a lot better than the last time I saw them."

Danny said, "Yeah, they look great. Let's see. At the restaurant that night we outlined all of the critical keys for products, so let me see what you came up with for the others."

He picked up each of the papers in turn, brought them closer and leaned back to study them. He looked pleased and nodded his head occasionally. Kevin and I waited as if expecting to receive message from the great Oz.

Finally he laid the images back down. "You guys did great. The critical keys that you identified are not exactly the same ones that we came up with, but that's understandable and it's fine. Our businesses and procedures are not identical. I'll show you ours one day, but for now and this discussion, I don't think we should change a thing."

I looked at Kevin and smiled. He was beaming, too.
"Sounds good." I said, "But now what the heck do we do with them?"

Stores on Fire

.

Chapter 14

Danny held up a hand as if to say, slow down. "Before we go there, I want you guys to set your goals using your real numbers."

"You mean with that calculator you demonstrated for me the other day?" I asked.

"Yep, that's what I mean. Like I said, we need to use your real numbers this time. Is your computer ready to go?"

"It's like the bunny ... ever ready," I said.

"OK, then enter www.discoveryretailgroup.com into your browser."

I did as he instructed, and after the site loaded I scanned down the page a little bit. I couldn't believe it.

"Oh my gosh," I exclaimed, pointing to the screen. "That book right there?"

"Yeah?" Danny questioned.

I opened a desk drawer, grabbed my copy of Discovery-Based Retail and tossed it to him. "One of my reps came in the other day and said he had heard these guys speak somewhere. He bought several copies of that book and he gave one of them to me."

"Well, I believe I'd keep that guy coming around," Danny said. "It's a very helpful book."

We discussed the book a few more minutes and then he said, "Let's get back at it. Hover over the 'resources tab' there in the top menu and you'll see a link that says "Incremental Improvement Calculator."

"OK, I see it."

"Go ahead and open it."

"You haven't installed people counters on your doors yet, have you?" he asked.

"No. It crossed my mind a couple times since we talked that day, but I haven't pulled the trigger."

"You need to get 'em coming. They're not real expensive,

maybe a couple hundred dollars a door or so. That would be the basic ones, but that's all you need. When people walk through their beams, the counter number increases."

"But, wouldn't it track them both ways?" Kevin asked. "You know, in and out?"

"Yeah, that type does, but it's no biggie. You just add up the totals for all the doors and divide by two to correct it. Providing no one spends the night, your numbers should be close," he laughed.

"What about employees going in and out?"

"Well, sure you're going to get some aberrations. For example, when a husband and wife come in together, they'll count as two people. But there probably wouldn't be two transactions. So your counts will always be variable. But the variables will all work together and eventually form a baseline. Your employees are going in and out every day, too, so they become part of that baseline. The important thing is that you work toward improvement. Another thing—as far as employees go, I wouldn't put counters on the doors that only the employees use for going out to the yard or into the stockroom. You'd get a lot of misinformation. I'd just use the counters for the primary doors, the ones that the customers use. How many of those are there?"

"Customers?" Kevin chuckled.

"Doors, Einstein, doors." Danny laughed, too.

"The front doors that you came through and then one on the side that some of the contractors use. You probably noticed it as we walked through the store," I said.

Danny nodded. "Then it'll be easy peasy. Two doors, two counters."

"We'll get that done," I said.

"OK. Good. So anyway, look at your screen here. See the top row of blue rectangles that already have some numbers in them?"

I nodded.

"We're going to take those numbers out and enter yours."

"Since we don't have an accurate customer count yet, we'll estimate that by using the numbers we do know. Eventually you'll have your counter numbers, but for right now, do you know how many transactions you average a day?"

"I think it's around 80." I said.

"OK. Remember I told you that my store's conversion rate was 63 percent when I started measuring it?"

I nodded.

He continued, "Let me use your calculator a second."

I passed it to him and after a few key strokes he said. "OK, put 127 in the cell under the one labeled 'Average Customer Count Per Day.'"

I did as he instructed. "Now, put 63 in the conversion rate cell."

After I did, he pointed at the screen and said, "Now you see that it says our average transaction count is 80?"

I nodded, and asked. "Can you see the screen OK, Kevin?"

"Yeah, boss, fine."

"That's just a guess using your transaction count and assuming your conversion rate is similar to what mine was before we started improving it. But, it's as close as we can get right now. What about your average transaction size?" Danny asked.

"I'll put in $60 again. That's very close," I said.

"OK, good. Now your margin goes in this cell."

"Kevin, what did we come up with on margin?"

"I think we checked and found it was 28 percent ... slightly under, but very close."

"Yes, you're right. So, I put 28 in here, right?"

"Yep. And I can't believe it, but you'll have to change the open 6 days a week to 5.5 for just a half day on Saturday," Danny said.

"You can't believe it?" I asked.

"Nope. I'll bet you have no idea why you're open five and half days a week instead of six. Do ya?"

"Not really. It's just the way it's always been done. Julie's dad said it didn't pay."

Average Customer Count Per Day	X	Average Conversion Rate	=	Average Transactions Per Day	X	Average Transactions Size	=	Average Daily Sales	X	Average Margin %	=	Average Margin $$ Per Day	X	Open Days Per Week
127	X	63.0%	=	80	X	60.00	=	$4,801	X	28.00%	=	$1,344	X	5.5
Planned Improvement	X	Planned Improvement	=	Average Transactions Per Day	X	Planned Improvement	=	Planned Improvement	X	Average Margin %	=	Average Margin $$ Per Day	X	Open Days Per Week

Amazing Results of Incremental Improvement

Current Gross Margin $$ Per Year	Targeted Gross Margin $$ Per Year	Gross Profit Dollars Improvement	Gross Profit Percentage Improvement
$384,432	$384,432	$0	0.0%

"We'll look into that later. Go ahead and change it to five and a half days."

I did and two cells of the calculator indicated that gross margin dollars produced were $384,432.

"Pass me the calculator again, would you please?"

I did. Danny pressed a few keys and said, "If these numbers are in the ball park then your sales were around a million seven hundred and fifty thousand. That seems like a lot more than we had at my office that day."

I remembered misleading Danny earlier and I don't know why. Even this time, at first, I hesitated giving the numbers in front of Kevin and then I quickly realized how silly my charades were. Talk about habits!

"Yeah, these numbers must be pretty darned close. They're spot on with last year's sales," I said.

Danny glanced at me, eyebrows raised. "OK, good, then it's time for you to start experimenting with goals."

He pointed to the screen. "You see this row in the black up here?"

Kevin and I both nodded.

"Notice that the variables of the opportunity equation are listed across there. See ... customer count, conversion rate, transaction size and margin? OK, down here in the blue cells is where we entered our proposed improvements. Remember?"

I nodded.

"Do you change the number?" Kevin asked.

"No. You enter the amount for your targeted improvement. So, for example, if you plan on increasing average daily customer count by two people, you'd enter a two in there."

"Ok, I see." Kevin said, and then quickly added. "Let's put more than two. I think we can do better than that."

"Me too."

"How many, do you think?" Danny asked.

I responded first. "I think five would be a good and reachable goal."

Kevin nodded.

"Ok, then put five in there," Danny said.

After I did, he pointed to the screen again. "See this number, $384,432, remained the same, but this cell now reads $399,567. The difference is indicated here; $15,135. That means if you increase your customer count by five people a day, like you said you thought you could, providing all of your other numbers remained the same, you'd produce that much more gross profit. And this cell indicates that that number would represent a 3.9 percent improvement."

Amazing Results of Incremental Improvement														
Average Customer Count Per Day	X	Average Conversion Rate	=	Average Transactions Per Day	X	Average Transactions Size	=	Average Daily Sales	X	Average Margin %	=	Average Margin $$ Per Day	X	Open Days Per Week
127	X	63.0%	=	80	X	60.00	=	$4,801	X	28.00%	=	$1,344	X	5.5
Planned Improvement	X	Planned Improvement	=	Average Transactions Per Day	X	Planned Improvement	=	Planned Improvement	X	Average Margin %	=	Average Margin $$ Per Day	X	Open Days Per Week
5.0		0.0%		0.00						0.00%				

Current Gross Margin $$ Per Year	Targeted Gross Margin $$ Per Year	Gross Profit Dollars Improvement	Gross Profit Percentage Improvement
$384,432	$399,567	$15,135	3.9%

I looked at Kevin. He was smiling, taking it all in.

We continued discussing the current numbers and how much improvement we should target. We ended up setting goals to improve our conversion rate by 5 percent, our transaction size by $1.50, and our margin by a point and a half. I felt good about all of them except maybe the margin. For us, margin was always a struggle, but Danny had a copy of the NRHA's Cost of Doing Business study with him. He pointed out that our resultant goal of a 29.5 percent margin would still be a little below the average for a typical home center. It was hard to argue with that, and especially when he told me that his store's margin was a bit over 31 percent.

"I suspect that our margin is lower because of our balance between inside and outside sales," I said.

"Yeah, maybe so," Danny offered. "But as you start improving things, that may shift enough to improve your margin even more than you're planning."

When I finished entering the numbers, I looked at the screen. Even though I had seen the demonstration before, I still found it hard to believe. It indicated that our gross margin dollars would increase by over $81,000 a year if we hit our goals!

"Would an extra eighty K help out around this joint?" Danny asked, smiling broadly.

"More than you know," I said. "More than you know."

Amazing Results of Incremental Improvement														
Average Customer Count Per Day	X	Average Conversion Rate	=	Average Transactions Per Day	X	Average Transactions Size	=	Average Daily Sales	X	Average Margin %	=	Average Margin $$ Per Day	X	Open Days Per Week
127	X	63.0%	=	80	X	60.00	=	$4,801	X	28.00%	=	$1,344	X	5.5
Planned Improvement	X	Planned Improvement	=	Average Transactions Per Day	X	Planned Improvement	=	Planned Improvement	X	Average Margin %	=	Average Margin $$ Per Day	X	Open Days Per Week
5.0	X	5.0%	=		X	1.50	=		X	1.50%	=		X	

Current Gross Margin $$ Per Year	Targeted Gross Margin $$ Per Year	Gross Profit Dollars Improvement	Gross Profit Percentage Improvement
$384,432	$465,743	$81,311	21.2%

***

There was electricity in the room, and I knew a lot of it was coming from me. I was excited, but still skeptical. So far I understood the four asset groups, the *Critical Keys*, and the huge improvements to our top line that would be created if we successfully improved the four elements of the opportunity equation, but now what?

"When are we going to find out what to do with all of this stuff?" I asked.

"Well, were going to start on that right now." Danny said. "Visualize the product asset group. Kevin, pull that image back out and lay it on the table."

Kevin did as instructed.

"OK you understand that these *Critical Keys* constantly cycle. But now visualize that there are other processes or tasks repeating inside of each critical key. Each of these holds the possibility for improvement. We call them *opportunity check points*. With some of them you may be operating at peak efficiency, but most of them can be improved. I brought along a list of the *opportunity check points* we made and used for the single *Critical Key* 'Buy them.'"

He reached into his briefcase and handed a paper to each of us. I glanced at it and saw that it contained questions and statements.

"Take a look at this and we'll go down the list of some of the ideas together. That'll help you understand what we're trying to achieve. Several of the *opportunity check points* are in the form of questions. That's the way we thought of them when we started our improvement process. I'll also explain the way we moved from the questions to actions. Sound good?" Danny asked.

Kevin nodded and I said, "Sounds awesome."

Danny continued, "OK the first question on the list is: Are you buying from multiple sources that could be combined into a single source or, at least, fewer sources?"

It seemed unremarkable to me. Danny must have read the reaction in my face and said, "Brother, we added some really good margin with this one and also shaved some payroll. Here's how we did it."

He seemed very focused, scooted closer to the table, and said, "We compiled a list of the vendors that we used regularly. We made notes of the products that we bought from each one. Once our list was completed, we checked for overlaps. When we found overlapping products, or products we could buy from our main hardware supplier instead of a local jobber, for example, we examined why. If we found valid reasons, say for example there was a brand that was only available through the jobber, we passed it. But mostly what we found is that there was no good reason to buy from many of the sources we were using. In the case of some the materials for the yard, we told our suppliers that we were going to concentrate our purchases. When we did that, each one really sharpened their pencils. We selected a primary supplier and it seemed that we were suddenly more important to them. We got concessions that we weren't getting when our purchases were diluted. It was a great move for us, and like I said, we added quite a bit of margin by the time we had completed the process."

"But if you didn't need the things that you were buying from the other distributors, why did you buy them in the first place?" I asked.

"You're missing the point. Of course, we needed the items that we were buying, but we didn't necessarily need to buy them from who we did. For example, if we were able to roll three suppliers into one, we spent less time ordering and less time processing freight. Our costs went down on many items, too, which drove our margin up. Does that make sense?" Danny asked.

"Yeah, I guess, but I still want to know why were you ordering from the other vendors in the first place?"

Danny chuckled, "Well we found that in a few cases it was because of allegiances to some good sales reps. I let one or two of those slide, but what we found in most cases was that it was just habit. We were doing it the way we were because it's the way we had always done it." He paused as if remembering the process and then added, "Habits are funny things. They allow us to complete tasks on autopilot, so in that regard, they're good. In that regard, they're time saving devices. But then again, in our store, there were processes, and I'm not talking about just buying things, that no one remembered how or why they were started. Those kinds of habits can be potentially bad and they need to be reexamined and shaken up."

Kevin joined in, "Oh, man, I think we've got a lot of that going on around here. You know, I've always wondered why we order the PVC fittings from Williams plumbing. We could bring them in with our regular hardware order and wouldn't miss a beat. It's a pain in the butt to work with their rep to get an order together. I like Joe OK, but really it is inconvenient. He seems to pop in at the most inopportune times and truthfully, he doesn't bring that much to the table. We have extra time involved in ordering, and then their stuff is always unpredictable as to when it will come in because it ships common carrier, and that causes us to be out of things more often than we should be."

"How does the pricing compare?" I asked.

He shrugged his shoulders. "I really have no idea. We order from him just because we always have. It's habit, just like Danny said."

I suddenly felt myself warming to the idea of going through the process just like Danny had described it.

"Go out there and ask Bobby to compare our costs on 10 random items that we buy from Williams. Have him compare them to our warehouse cost, would you Kevin?"

"Now?"

"Yeah, just get him working on it. I'm really curious to know now."

"Sure, boss, no problem."

As Kevin left the room I turned back toward Danny and asked, "OK, so we just list all of our suppliers and what we buy from each one. Is that right?"

"Yeah, and when you see them listed you'll have questions immediately. I'll bet on it."

I nodded. "You ready for a Coke or a cup of coffee? I'm buying."

"Sure, let's take a break."

Chapter 15

After thirty minutes or so, we made our way back to my office.

Danny and I were already seated when Kevin walked in and handed me a sheet of paper.

"What's this?" I asked.

"It's the price comparison that I had Bobby do. I think it's going to shock you," he said, grimacing, eyebrows raised.

"That was fast!" I offered.

When I glanced at it, the comparison did surprise me. We were paying a premium of around 20 percent over what we could buy the products for from our warehouse, some items even more, and although the fittings were not expensive, percentage wise it was a big difference. I passed the sheet to Danny and he studied it carefully.

"This is the same kind of thing we found. And, in some cases, truthfully, it was even worse." He passed the sheet back to me.

I guess it may sound kind of crazy, but, honestly, I felt a little violated. I suddenly understood what Danny had been trying to communicate. Incremental improvements in enough areas and we would certainly achieve the margin increase that we targeted. Suddenly my skepticism evaporated. I was now totally on board. So, this is what management looks like, I thought.

I turned toward Kevin and said, "Not right this moment, but make a note to have Bobby or Terrance get SKU numbers from the warehouse for all of the products that we've been buying from Williams. Have Sherry add them to the computer; tell her to keep the Williams numbers, too. Double check them yourself just to make sure that we don't miss anything, and then you and I will set reorder points and quantities later. Starting this week, let's just roll those items in to our regular warehouse order."

He nodded and said, "OK, but what do I tell Joe?"

I thought for a moment and quickly decided I wouldn't push the dirty work off on Kevin. "Have him come talk to me. I'll tell him what we're doing and why."

Kevin looked relieved and nodded confirmation.

I looked at Danny. He smiled and said, "One caution, and this is very important: make sure that your retails stay the same so the savings you realize will go to increase margin. Unless, of course, you've been getting price resistance in the category. That would be a different story, but I doubt that you do with those types of fittings."

"Good point," I said.

"Yeah." He continued, "But otherwise. congratulations and Cha-ching. Your first incremental margin improvement. Remember—all of the time your staff used to order and process freight from vendors you pare is freed up for something else. Improvements like this are what I'm talking about when I say 'incremental increases.' You'll be driving margin up and, possibly, payroll down."

I nodded. "Yeah, I get it now. I'm excited. So, what's next on your list?"

"Well, it's kind of related, but slightly different. This is the question we asked: 'Have you recently verified that the pricing you are receiving is as it was originally represented?'"

Kevin jumped in, "I don't really get that one."

"Well, for example, in our store, we sell boxed nails instead of offering them by the pound."

"Us too," Kevin answered.

"When we originally decided on a supplier," Danny said, "We had four different vendors give us bids. We went with the best prices at the time. Once they were in stock and habits were established we forgot about them. We used a business-as-usual approach and defaulted to habit. When we started our incremental improvement process I had the other three vendors bid them again. I found that the one we originally contracted with had raised their prices over time. It was gradual so it flew under our radar. But during the recheck we found that two of the other vendors were lower, and one of them actually saved us about 8 percent. They bought out our existing stock so it allowed us to clean things up and that really helped, too. But this time I was a little smarter; I told the new vendor that we were going to verify our pricing monthly. We don't get it done every month probably, but each time we've checked prices they've still been right in line. Funny thing though, the old vendor came back in and told us they would beat our new lower prices, but I didn't fall for it this time. They weren't going to fool me twice. Anyway, with the number of nails we sell, that was a *big* win for us."

"Couldn't you just bring the nails in from your hardware supplier?" Kevin asked.

Danny looked taken aback and hesitated before answering. "Yeah, we could I suppose, but originally in our case they weren't as competitive as our building material suppliers. You might find it otherwise, but the point is to explore your options and then periodically check back in on your decisions."

Danny paused again, appeared to be deep in thought and then finally said, "You know what though? We didn't actually check their price when we went through the reexamination. I don't know why we didn't. So, I'm going to do as you suggested and check our hardware vendor, too. It would really be sweet to buy the nails from them if it worked out so we could. Wow, talk about habits. We had always bought nails from one of our building materials suppliers, so that's where we looked."

I could read the satisfaction on Kevin's face as Danny

scribbled a reminder in his pocket notebook. Kevin got even bolder and added, "You'll have to factor in your rebate, too."

Danny glanced up, smiled and asked, "What's this? The student teaching the master?"

We were all amused, but while the fun jabs were being exchanged, I wrote a reminder of Kevin's observation in my notes.

"I can't think of many lines that we originally took bids on like that. Nails, of course, but beyond that I'm not sure," I said.

Kevin responded quickly. "Some of them may have been done before you even arrived," he said. "We originally took bids on some paint sundries, but man, that's been a long time ago. But after the first point we discussed I had already made a note to check the pricing on those."

"Yeah, the two points do kind of overlap," Danny offered. "But in our pass with the first question we didn't include the nails because we felt we had already verified the prices."

Kevin nodded, looked at me and then said, "Welding supplies, grills, insecticides and fertilizers, vinyl moldings, door sweeps and weather-stripping, builders hardware ..."

I held up my hand. "OK, I get it, I get it. Welding supplies weren't even available from the warehouse at the time we added them, but I think they are now. As far as the insecticides and fertilizers, I don't think we'd want to change vendors there. People really like the brands we have."

Kevin agreed.

"Sure. Make decisions on each line, but do so consciously and deliberately," Danny said.

I nodded understanding, made a few more notes, and then said, "OK, what's the next question on the list?"

"It's kind of two parts ... two questions," Danny said.

Kevin and I nodded. We were fully engaged in the conversation.

"Are you paying a premium for buying quantities less than full units? That's the first part. And the next question is: Are there price concessions for buying larger quantities?"

"Kind of sounds like the same question to me," Kevin said.

Danny bobbed his head from side to side. "Well, yes and no, but not really. Say, for example, a paint brush is packed in cartons of 12 and at that quantity they're 4 percent cheaper. You buy 6 at a time. Maybe you're sacrificing that 4 percent in order to improve turns. Turns are important, but I've come to realize that I don't deposit turns. So we went through and looked for places where we could improve margin by bumping up quantities to full cartons. We found a lot of opportunities."

"But, didn't your inventory go up?" I asked.

"Yeah, that's the down side; the up side is that our sales did, too."

I must have looked puzzled because momentarily he answered my unspoken question. "I think our turn-focused approach to inventory was causing us to miss some sales. Sure, we knew that if we had an "out of stock" we were missing sales. But we weren't aware that if we didn't have sufficient stock for customers to complete their jobs, they wouldn't even buy the items we did have. They just went somewhere else to buy it all. After we beefed up inventory, we became the place where people could come to 'buy it all.' It made a huge difference."

"OK, that makes sense," Kevin said. "But I don't get the second half of the question and how it's different. Are there price concessions for buying larger quantities ... sounds like the same thing."

"Yeah I see why it would, but here's what I mean. We were already buying full cases of paint thinner two or three at a time and reordering regularly. That was full cartons. My department manager pointed out that we could get some pretty good savings buying it by the pallet. Once we started doing that it was easy to see that we were turning it regularly enough for the pallet to be a great investment. We display most of it in a power aisle by just leaving it on the pallet at regular price. Sometimes if we find ourselves looking for an item for an endcap, we can always fall back to paint thinner. I don't like to, because I hate promoting commodities, but there's always plenty in stock. It was a 'no-brainer move' in hindsight."

Kevin and I were feverishly taking notes. We didn't want to miss a thing.

While we were writing, Danny began talking again. "Another thing we started as a result of our process is that I had everybody in each department write down in notebooks things that people asked for that we were out of. Our computer system would let us know if we were out of stock, but the lists gave us clues as to how many sales we missed because of it. After we started this process and I became more aware, it infuriated me. We used that information to help us establish better mins and maxes, and it also lead us back to buying in full packs and bigger quantities."

"Mins and Maxes?" Kevin asked.

"Yeah, your system calls them reorder points and quantities, I think," Danny said.

"Oh gotcha."

"Oh, and the other thing we did later," Danny said, "was to have the department personnel record everything that they were asked for that we didn't stock at all. If an item showed up once, it was no big deal. But you'd be surprised how many items we added that were asked for multiple times. Some of those items have been really good for us."

"That's a great idea," I said.

***

We continued down Danny's list. We discussed buying-shows and market opportunities, pallet quantities and marketing calendars. By this time it was middle of the afternoon. We hadn't eaten yet and it seemed that we were all beginning to drag.

"When do you have to be back, Danny?" I asked.

He glanced at his watch. "You know what? I really need to be going now. I'm supposed to go to a party tonight, don't really want to, but I need to."

I nodded. "Do you have time to grab a late lunch?" I asked. "We're buying."

He looked at his watch again, shook his head reluctantly, and said, "Nah, probably not. I think I'll just swing in to a drive through and grab a burger or something."

He patted his stomach, smiled broadly and added, "You don't build one of these babies by eating soups and salads."

We laughed and made inappropriate comments the way we had become accustomed to doing with each other. After that, we concluded that Kevin and I had plenty to keep us busy. We agreed that since we had a good idea of how the process worked now, we would try our luck at listing *opportunity check points* for the next *Critical Key.*

After we walked with Danny to the front to let him out, Kevin and I hung around the cash wrap talking about what we had learned.

"Pull up sales for today, how did we do?" I asked.

Kevin keyed in codes and was soon looking at the sales journal. "Gosh, look at this," he said.

I moved around the counter so that I could see the screen. "Wow, that's the best Saturday we've had in a long time."

"I don't remember a better one," Kevin said. "Why do you think that was?"

I shook my head. "I have no idea, but I'll be anxious to talk to everyone and see what they have to say."

Chapter 16

Saturday had been a great, productive day. I was a bit tired when I walked into the house early that evening, but I knew I had to get over it quickly when I saw Julie. She was excited about something and that was easy to see.

"I want to hear all about your day," she said. But before I could say anything, she continued. "I hope you're not too tired, I kind of have something planned for us," she grinned mischievously.

"Planned for us?"

"Yeah, I'm sorry." She wrinkled her cute little nose. "I had to make a decision, and you told me not to disturb you today if I didn't have to."

She had me there. I had told her not to interrupt my meeting with Danny unless it was absolutely necessary.

"OK?" I held the question with ascending tone.

"We're going out," she exclaimed, animated, beaming.

"With whom?" I asked.

"With Chance and Maria. They asked us to go out to dinner with them, and then they wanted to know if we'd go dancing, too. I said 'yes.'" She giggled like a school girl.

Well look who's back, I thought.

"Sure. It sounds like fun. I'm a little tired, but after a shower, I'll be ready to take my best girl out dancing."

She played along. "So, I'm the best, but you have others, is that it?"

I smiled. "Nope, more than I can handle right here."

She winked. "Well, we'll see about that after dinner and dancing."

She glanced at her watch. You'd better hurry; they're going to pick us up in about 45 minutes.

***

The girls had decided that Palmer's Steak House was a good choice for dinner, and, you know how it goes—what the girls want, the girls get. We were fortunate to be seated at a booth that afforded a nice view of Briley park. It was approaching dusk, but as the lights sprang to life, the scene became even more enchanting, kind of like a fairy-tale book image.

We ordered drinks and appetizers. As I recall, we spent a bit of time discussing the latest hot community gossip. Mayor Jackson was being "encouraged" to resign by a group of "concerned citizens" about town. It seems that rumored improprieties had surfaced. He and a local minister's wife were allegedly having midnight communions, if you know what I mean. For whatever reason, after a couple of drinks, the tragedy of it all was replaced, in our minds, by humorous view points and in our mouths with crude one-liners. Yeah, I know, it was sick, but what can I say?

Anyway, while we were talking and laughing a guy walks up to our table. He reached out to shake my hand and said, "Hey Charlie, I don't know if you remember me. My name is Mike Langley."

"Sure, Mike. I remember you, Langley Construction, right?" He nodded as I continued, "It's been a long time since I've seen you." (I couldn't even remember the last time he had been in the store.)

"Yeah, it's been a while. Hey, listen, I was in your store today. I didn't see you, but I just wanted to let you know that your people did a great job of taking care of me."

"Well, that's good to hear. Where have you been? Just didn't have any projects going?" I asked.

He looked away, sheepishly. "No, that wasn't it, I stay busy all the time. To tell you the truth, I just quit coming in. I've been going to Builders' Market."

I felt a twinge of pain in my gut as I responded, "Listen

this may not be the best place for this, but do you mind if I ask why?"

"Well, I'd rather not talk about the why." He looked uncomfortable, stumbled with his words and then hesitated before continuing. "I don't want to say anything bad about anybody. But, anyway, I heard through the grapevine that you've been changing some personnel, and I heard that you had promoted a couple people. So," he shrugged his shoulders before continuing, "I just wanted to see for myself so I dropped in."

I studied his face. I could tell that it hadn't been easy for him to approach me. He could probably tell that it wasn't the easiest conversation for me either. I felt he had been forthright and honest with me so I felt compelled to reciprocate.

"Thank you, Mike. We're trying to get things squared away. Truthfully, I had never managed a business before. The accident forced me into it." He nodded in acknowledgement as I continued. "I'm trying hard to learn to run the place better, and frankly, I need your business. Heck, I need all the business I can get."

I don't know where that came from, but it felt good to ask for his business and I thought it resonated with him.

He smiled. "Well, listen, I don't want to interrupt your meal, I just wanted you to know that I had dropped in."

"Will you be coming back?" I asked, almost afraid to hear his answer.

"Yeah, I think so. In fact, I've got a new home that I'm going to start in a few weeks up near Mill Creek. I'll drop by with the plans, and maybe we can discuss it. I would prefer doing business with a hometown owner if it works."

"Mike, I really appreciate it. We'll try our best to make it work."

He smiled, nodded, and said, "OK, sounds good. I'll talk to you soon." then turned and walked away.

I turned back to face Chance. I didn't know exactly how to react, so I raised my eyebrows, pursed my lips and shrugged my shoulders.

Chance watched me closely and appeared to be thinking about his words before saying, "You know, he's not the only one, don't you?"

"What do you mean?" I said, puzzled.

"There are a lot of people that quit coming to your store, because frankly, it hasn't been a very pleasant place to shop. They were often treated rudely, and to tell you truth, most people won't put up with it. You told me once that you were working on lowering prices because you thought that was your main problem; it wasn't."

I was a little more than irritated. I was pissed. "And why in the hell didn't you say something to me before now?"

He shrugged his shoulders, "I kind of tried in a round-a-bout way, but you didn't seem to want to listen to anybody. I guess you're listening now to this guy you met in Arkansas, but no one else before, that I'm aware of."

I suddenly felt thankful to have a friend that would shoot this straight with me. I went quiet as I thought about what he had said. He continued to study me and I could tell that he hoped I would hear his message and understand his intent. I did. He was trying to be helpful. I thought back to conversations we had had. He ran a very successful business, but, after all, it was only a machine shop. Really, what correlations would there be? Then it hit me; there were many similarities, not the least of which were how people were made to feel when they were in your store.

"I didn't intend to hurt your feelings," he finally said.

I breathed deeply to steady myself and then replied. "I think it's more a bruised ego than feelings. But I appreciate your honesty."

"Running a business isn't easy," he continued with a bob of the head and shrug of the shoulders. "But I really believe you're on the right track."

***

"That was so much fun!" Julie said as she reached to turn the bed side light off. "Did you think it was fun?" she asked.

"Yeah, I had a good time and I think Chance and Maria did, too. My only problem was that my mind kept thinking back to my conversation with Mike. But when we started dancing I got over it."

Julie snuggled closer. "Dancing was so much fun. How long had it been since we went dancing?"

I thought it rhetorical or at least I didn't know the answer. She quickly continued, "You're doing a great job at the store now. You've just got to stay focused. When do you meet with Danny again?"

"We haven't really set a date yet. Kevin and I have a lot to work on before the next time."

"But you know how to move forward, right?"

"Yeah. The next few steps are pretty clear. We accomplished a lot today." I paused a moment before continuing, "Oh, by the way, do you have anything planned for tomorrow?"

"Not really. I may spend part of the day cleaning the house, but then again, it's Sunday, so I may not," she giggled. "Why, is there something that you want to do?"

"I was thinking about going down to the yard for a couple hours in the morning. I want to make some notes and plan for the week, and it'll be easier to do without distractions."

"Wow, you're energized by the changes you're making aren't you?"

I thought about it for a moment and then said, "Yes. It's suddenly becoming more fun than drudgery."

"That's awesome."

I was starting to drift off when she said, "Charlie, what was that you were saying today about having more than you could handle right here? Let's do a fact check on that."

Chapter 17

Monday morning began with a bang. Kevin and I discussed reviewing the sourcing and pricing on other product lines. We decided to follow the strategy as Danny had outlined. I spoke with every employee who worked that Saturday morning. I wanted to give them all a pat on the back and get their opinions about what had led to the improved results. The feedback was a mixed bag, but to a person, they spoke about less stress on the sales floor. Brad's name came up several times, but I found it hard to believe that one person could make that much difference.

Bobby's explanation was probably the most telling. He said, (I am paraphrasing here), that Brad was always griping about or criticizing something, including the store, me and other employees. He said Brad was unpleasant with customers and acted like they were a bother to him. He also mentioned that since Kevin's promotion, directions had been clearer. He said that he and the other employees felt that they had a much better idea of what was expected of them.

He seemed almost afraid to mention those things. Maybe he thought I would take his words as personal criticism, but I assured him that I was glad to hear honest feedback. When I explained that it would help us move forward and improve the store, he seemed to like that. He recalled that Mike Langley had stopped by and bought a few things. He said several other people that he hadn't seen for a while were in, too. He guessed it was just "one of those days" when people, for whatever reason, were just out and about. I told him that I had seen Mike at the restaurant over the weekend, and that we might actually get a chance to do more business with him. He seemed genuinely excited to hear it.

Around 11:00 that morning UPS delivered the customer counters that I had ordered a few days earlier. I called Kevin to my office and asked if there was anybody available to install them.

"I've got everybody working on other things right now." He opened the package to study the installation instructions and then said, "I don't think it'll take that long to put them up. They're battery powered so we don't have to worry about getting electricity to them, right?"

"Yeah, I think so, the information said they could be installed either way. There was a transformer available, but I didn't order it. I thought we'd just put them up using batteries, and see how long they last. If the batteries go bad too fast, we'll buy the transformers."

"Ok, sounds good. I can install them myself, I guess," he said.

I glanced at Kevin and considered it an opportunity to promote teamwork, "Tell you what. Let's go out there and we'll do it together. I don't think it'll take us 30 minutes."

It didn't; 20 minutes later we were counting customers.

After we finished with that, Kevin went to follow up on the tasks he had assigned. I went back to my office to review the notes I had made during my private think session on Sunday. It wasn't a long list, but as I glanced at it, I remembered I had written and underlined this phrase; *Change the Culture.*

The chance meeting with Mike Langley Saturday night had made an impression on me. You've probably already gathered that. As I considered it on Sunday I came to this conclusion: I could change processes and I would. The system that Danny was exposing us to would help us with that. But even if the systems were in place and the processes were established, if they weren't delivered with a customer-centric focus, our efforts would fail, or at the very least, would never reach optimum potential. Even one person with a bad attitude could undermine any effort and improvements we made. As I visualized how that process might occur my mind formed an image of a cancer cell invading an otherwise healthy body and slowly growing to the point that it diseased the entire host. It seems that for much too long I had overlooked one such cell.

Change the Culture; it seemed a simple enough concept, but what would it look like? How would it function? And, how would we move toward it.

***

While I was reading the rest of my notes, the phone rang. I noticed the caller ID and quickly picked it up.

"Hey, Danny. Did you make it back in time for your party?" I asked.

"Hey, brother. Oh, hell yeah, but I'm tellin' ya' I could of done without it," he laughed gregariously. "I made it, alright, and I survived it, too. Anyway, how you doing? I'm just checking in to see if you've had a chance to think about the things we discussed on Saturday and to see if you've got any questions."

I told him that I had thought a lot about the meeting. I brought him up to speed on the additional cost examinations we were planning. I told him about the sales spike on Saturday and my conversation with Mike Langley that evening. I relayed Chance's comment about the community recognizing that we had made some personnel changes and the favorable reaction there had been. Then I told him about my Sunday think session and that I was reviewing the notes I had made.

"Were you starting to work on *opportunity check points* for one of the other *Critical Keys?*"

"No, not yet. Kevin and I are going to do that together. I just wanted to take some time to think about everything we've discussed so far. You know ... review my notes and get it all straight in my head. But then, for whatever reason, I wrote this down: "Change the Culture" and I even underlined it. When I started my review this morning that caught my eye, and that's what I was thinking about when you called. I don't know, it just seemed that it's going to be an important factor if we are really going to improve things and push forward." I paused for what seemed like a long time.

"And?" he asked.

"I don't know." Although he couldn't have seen it, I shrugged my shoulders. "It just occurred to me that the systems and examinations that you're helping us with are important, but if they exist in an environment that doesn't provide good customer experiences, we're probably thinking about managing receipts that we're not even producing."

I could hear Danny chuckle, and for a moment I wished I hadn't shared.

"What's so funny?" I asked.

"It's not really funny, brother, it's just that you're picking up on this stuff so fast. Faster than I did, that's for sure. Ah hell, wait a minute, I take it back, it is funny. In fact, it strikes me as damned funny that you don't even recognize how far you've come already."

After hearing that comment, I was feeling better about where the conversation was going and asked, "So, tell me then, how do I change the culture of the store?"

"You've already begun to, brother. You've had a store meeting or two coaching up employees and outlining expectations. You've purged a bad employee. You've interacted with employees regarding sales results. You've appointed a second-in-command to act on your behalf and increase the communication of your expectations. You've begun visualizing a brighter future. You've started implementing the *incremental improvement system* which will improve your profitability. You've asked at least one customer for his business. You've installed customer counters to provide valuable information for your push toward better results. Brother, you are already changing the culture, and it seems to me that you're doing it at warp speed."

I considered what he was saying, "But what about customer experience?"

"You've begun to improve that, too, but think about this: the Four Asset Groups of the Incremental Improvement System are, Inventory, Facility, Employees and what?"

"Customers."

"Bingo, little brother, bingo. They all work together. The process helps you drill down on building better customer experiences, too. But, here's something that goes beyond the boundaries of the system: store experience improvement is a top-down process."

"Top-down?' I puzzled.

"Yeah, in your store's case, it starts with you. You are the role model in your store, and in stores where managers run the operations instead of owners, they're the role models. I really think the store takes on the owner's or the manager's personality. That's in everything from creating a fun and attractive environment to dealing with people."

"So, you're saying that if my store produced an unpleasant environment for customers it was because of me?"

Danny was silent.

"Ok, forget I asked," I said. "I get it."

.

Chapter 18

The next couple of weeks flew by. By that time we were fully engaged and focused on making positive changes. Don't get me wrong, not everything went smoothly and according to plan, but many things did. We continued our review of pricing and ultimately decided to terminate seven vendors. We hadn't done tons of business with any of them, but the changes did cause noticeably larger warehouse orders. Kevin reviewed the shortages and damages reports we had filed with our hardware provider over the previous six months. Based on what he found, we decided to do as Danny had suggested and move the freight directly to the sales floor. I was blown away at how much time we saved with these two simple changes; consolidation of vendors and bypassing the check-in process. My uneasiness over the changes was decreased when I soon realized just by placing the merchandise on the shelves we could still quickly spot check quantities and audit for damages. Kevin leveraged the labor savings we produced to make improvements on the floor.

He walked in to my office one Wednesday afternoon for the meeting that had now become our routine. "OK," he said. "Do you want to take a guess at our conversion rate?"

"Oh, wow, I had forgotten about installing the counters. Yeah, I guess I'll stick with my original 67 percent ... or did I say 63? Heck, I don't remember. OK, I'll go with 67."

Kevin smiled and shook his head back and forth. "Better or worse?" I asked.

"A little worse, but not much," he waited.

"OK, I'll switch to my other guess then. Sixty-three percent."

"Sixty Five, so you were close."

"Yeah, I think that's about what we originally guessed it

to be, but now we've got a benchmark for improvement. Do you remember what number we set for our improvement target on that calculator thing Danny showed us?" I asked.

"No, but I've got it here in my notes somewhere." He turned several pages in a yellow covered spiral notebook. "Yeah, here it is. We used 63 percent for our starting point because that's what Danny said his was when he started. Then, we set a goal of selling another 5 out of 100 people who come in. So that would bring it to 68 percent."

I thought about it for a moment and then said, "OK, let's leave our initial goal at 68 percent because it already feels like we've made some progress. It may already be higher than it was, you know? Anyway, when we reach 68 we'll revisit it."

"OK," said Kevin. "And I agree with you. It does feel like we're making progress. I don't know if it would show as increased conversion rate or not. We haven't measured it long enough to know, but people are noticing a difference in our store. I'm certain of that."

I was nodding in agreement as my intercom buzzed. It was Sherry. "Charley, sorry to bother you but there is a Mr. Fletcher on the phone. He says he's from the bank. Do you want to take it or ..."

Feeling instantly uneasy in my gut, I interrupted. "Yeah, Sherry I'll take it. Thanks."

I glanced at Kevin, raised my eyebrows and grimaced as I answered, "Hi Clancy, how ya' doing?"

"I'm good, Charlie, you doing OK?"

There was likely a quiver in my voice as I answered. "Yeah, I think so. What's up?"

"Well, I read the note you wrote on your email the other day when you sent the numbers I requested. I want to hear more about the changes you're making. But, the main reason for my call is I'd like to see how you're progressing against the budget numbers you set at the first of the year."

I paused. I didn't want to meet with him. Could I please choose between this and plucking an eyeball out? Thinking about it was already making me queasy. Then again, I knew I had no choice. "Sure, Clancy. When do you want to get together?"

"I could make some time this afternoon, or tomorrow. Tell me which works best for you."

If he's in this big of a hurry I thought, this must be serious. "Today is kind of already booked. (I lied) How about tomorrow afternoon?" (I needed all the time I could get.)

"That'll work." He said, "Say 2:30?"

"Ok, I'll see you then."

We exchanged pleasantries and I hung up the phone.

Kevin studied me carefully. "Everything OK, boss?"

"Time will tell, I guess. That was Clancy down at the bank; he wants to meet with me tomorrow. Maybe it's nothing, it's just unusual, that's all."

Kevin nodded acknowledgement. He looked worried, too.

"Listen, Kevin, maybe we'd better postpone our meeting today. I need to get some things together for that meeting."

"Alright boss. If there's anything I can do to help, let me know."

I told him I would and watched as he disappeared into the hallway.

***

I searched through my computer files for the budget I had thrown together at the beginning of the year. Just between me and you, I really hadn't paid much attention to it since a month or two after I put it together. I saw at that time that we weren't on course to hit the sales or expense targets, but I didn't know what to do about it or what the implications were, so it was easier to ignore it. Now here I was, as the old timers might say, 'in a pickle.' I didn't have any idea how to balance what I had forecasted against where we were. Panic flooded over me, but then, in a moment of clarity, I decided to call Danny and ask his advice.

He answered quickly. "Hey buddy, what's up? You been working on your Incremental Improvement Plan?"

"Yeah, we have, but listen Danny, I've got a situation and I want to pick your brain to see how you would handle it," I said.

"Pick away, brother. Whatcha got?"

I told him about Clancy's call and explained that the meeting was scheduled for the next day.

"How did you formulate your budget?" he asked.

"I just took last year's numbers and added a bit to the sales, I guess."

"Based on what?" He asked.

"A WAG, I guess."

"WAG?"

"Yeah, you know. I wild-ass guess."

He ignored my comment and then rattled off, "How much profit would you end up with if you hit all of your budgeted numbers, how would that compare to last year and how are you doing in relationship to those numbers right now?"

I was quiet as a rock. I knew I was in deep trouble.

"You still there?" he eventually asked.

"Yeah, I am, but I'm beginning to wish I wasn't."

He sensed my uneasiness.

"OK, listen, take a deep breath and let's think about this. What did he say exactly?"

I retold the story including as much detail as I could recall.

"OK, we'll talk about budgeting later, because you really need to get that taken care of. A budget should be dynamic, reviewed monthly and serve as a road guide for steering your efforts."

I was more than just a little annoyed and blurted out disgustedly, "Yeah, yeah, yeah but what about tomorrow?"

He laughed and replied, "Whoa' there partner. I'm on your side, remember?"

I regained my composure and instantly felt bad about the way I had reacted. "Danny, I'm sorry. I really am. That was BS. I plead temporary insanity. "

He laughed again. "No problem, little brother, chill. I thought you were going to sing a Beatles song there for a moment."

"Uh?"

"Bad joke. You said yeah, yeah, yeah, as in she loves you, yeah, yeah...." He paused, but I had nothin', so he eventually continued. "Listen, son, you got this. Go in there and try to control the conversation. Explain to him what you've learned, what you're focusing on and what you expect to gain from it. Don't bring up the budget unless he does."

"And if he does ... when he does?" I asked.

"Well, I assume he's already seen your original budget, right?"

"Yeah, at the beginning of the year."

"Well then take another copy of that and if he asks about it, just hand it to him. If he asks how you're doing on it, tell him that you're making headway with your improvements."

"Sounds elusive and a bit like double-talk," I said.

"Maybe, but your main objective should be to try to put him at ease. Remember that. Remember also, that you're in a much better place than you were a few weeks ago, so focus on that. Let him feel your optimism."

For some reason, it all seemed to resonate. Suddenly, in that moment, I felt as if I could handle things just as he had suggested.

We had a few more moments of casual conversation which I don't recall. But, I knew I had to get busy, so I said, "Hey Danny, I really appreciate you and I apologize again for flyin' off the handle a while ago."

"Oh, no biggie. I understand you're feeling pressured, but believe me, it's temporary. Call me when your meeting is over, OK?"

"Will do. Thanks again."

Chapter 19

My palms were sweating profusely as I walked into the bank at precisely 2:25 the following day. I could hear my footsteps reverberating in the high ceilings and beams as I walked across the polished marble floor. I think I could hear my heart beating, too. I had rehearsed and visualized the meeting repeatedly, but the calm I had experienced after consulting with Danny hadn't lasted. I don't know where it went, but I didn't take it to the bank that afternoon. I tried to focus on doing as Danny had suggested and see myself controlling the direction of the conversation, but the uncertainties kept sneaking in.

A receptionist at the centrally located service desk greeted me. "May I help you?" She had a pleasing smile which on a normal day would have been calming.

"Sure thing. I've got an appointment with Clancy, I believe it's for 2:30." (I had already decided I would address Clancy by his first name.)

"Oh, Ok, I'll let Mr. Fletcher know you're here. May I give him your name?"

"Charlie, Charlie Kern."

"Please have a seat anywhere you like, Mr. Kern, and I'll let him know you're here." She made a sweeping gesture toward the chairs lining the room. "Would you like something to drink while you wait?"

"Nah, I don't think so. But, thanks anyway."

I couldn't make out her side of the short conversation from where I sat, but within a minute or two Clancy walked out of a corner office.

He greeted me with a broad smile, firm handshake and thick southern accent. "Hi Charlie, good to see you. Thank you for coming. I've been hearin' good things about you and your store the last few weeks."

Where did that come from, I wondered; not at all what I expected. Somehow my confidence crept back in. "Thanks, Clancy. I think we're really gaining on things." I shrugged my shoulders and added, "But I do appreciate you saying that."

"Why, certainly, Charley; certainly. Come on back." He made a guiding gesture and added, "Let's go down this way. I'm anxious to hear what you guys have been doing out there."

I followed Clancy down a long hallway lined with beautifully polished red oak. He eventually stepped to the side and motioned for me to enter a brightly-lit room on the right. It contained a single round meeting table and six comfortable-looking black leather chairs. I glanced at the inspiring messages written on pictures and plaques lining the windowless walls.

"Sit anywhere you like, Charley. I thought we'd use this room instead of my office because it's kind of a mess, you know? Anyway this room is nice for visitin'"

I selected a chair, sat down, and watched as Clancy positioned himself across from me. "Did April offer you somethin' to drink while you were waitin'?"

"Yes she did. Thank you."

"Well sure, Charley. No problem."

He asked about Julie, and I reciprocated by inquiring about his family, although truthfully I knew little about them.

After a few moments of casual conversation, he opened the meeting by saying, "Charley, like I told you on the phone yesterday, I want to learn about the things you mentioned that you've been workin' on to improve your operation. And then, I want to see how you're doin' with your budget, too." He was nodding his head rhythmically as he spoke.

I answered quickly. "Great! I've been wanting to bring you up to speed. We're pretty excited about the store." (The first part of my statement was a lie ... the second part wasn't.)

"We're?"

"I'm sorry?" I asked.

"You said *we're* excited. Who are you referrin' to exactly?" He leaned his chair back, placed the tips of his fingers together and brought them to his pursed lips.

"My whole team," I paused momentarily before continuing. "Me and my employees."

(Man, did it ever feel good to say that!)

"I see. Well, good. Go ahead and tell me about that."

"I don't know if you've heard or not, but I promoted Kevin. You know Kevin Conley, don't you?"

"I'm aware of him, but that's about all, I'm afraid. He's worked out there for a long time, hasn't he?"

"Yeah, he has. Long before me; even before Julie's parents bought the place. Anyway, I made him assistant manager. That's been a real good move. And, I've been doing a much better job of using his experience and abilities. He's really surprised me."

"That's good, but" Clancy raised a pointing finger for emphasis, "Just be cautious. Payroll is the largest number on most businesses' expense statements, includin' yours. Once it's high, it's hard to get a handle on it, and it's never popular to roll it back, so just tread carefully."

I knew it was true, so I responded. "You're exactly right and so we're making some changes to try to reduce our payroll demand."

"Your payroll demand?" He asked.

"Yeah, we're streamlining some processes," I continued. Then I told him about paring vendors and the procedural changes we had undertaken. I outlined the labor savings we had already realized through those efforts and then concluded with. "We're really focused on increasing the employee productivity gap."

"Tell me what you mean by that," he said.

"It's just a ratio, I guess; anyway that's how I think of it. If I pay an employee $500, then how much profit does that employee produce for me? The more we can widen that gap, the gap between what I pay them and what they produce, the better. So we're focusing on product and sales training, communication, inclusion, team building, cross-training and those sorts of things. We're using store meetings to bring everybody up to higher standards." (I didn't mention that we'd only had a couple of them.)

"So you're speaking about payroll productivity, I guess."

"Yeah, sort of. But payroll productivity is a backward-looking assessment. If we focus on *creating* bigger productivity gaps we're much more tuned in to coaching everybody up and making positive changes. The payroll productivity ratio would then look back and measure our success. Does that make any sense?"

"Absolutely," he said as he leaned back in his chair again, removed his glasses, and began chewing at the plastic covering on the ear pieces. I watched him closely as I waited. He appeared to be processing what he had just heard. Momentarily he added, "Now that's the kinds of things I've been wantin' to hear."

"Well, talking about payroll expense, and expenses in general for that matter, I understand the need to closely monitor them. But, now I'm going to contradict myself; we can't make any more headway unless we shift our focus away from cutting expenses."

Clancy looked puzzled. "You kind of lost me there, Charley."

"Cutting expenses is what the store has focused on for years, and you can see where that's gotten us. So, we've shifted our focus to increasing top-line. We're concentrating on improving the four variables that can increase it."

"Four variables?"

I felt confident by this point. Danny had been right; I had this. "Yes, we're working on strategies to improve our customer count, our conversion rate, our margin and our transaction size."

"That's interesting, Charlie. What made you decide to place your attention there?"

I went on to explain how those four elements affect top-line and how dramatic even small changes could be. I talked about conversion rate and why it's important. I'm gonna level with you; I didn't mention that I had become acquainted with Danny or anything about him teaching us this stuff. In fact, I guess I implied that the ideas were original and that Kevin and I were the genesis for the new strategies. It wasn't that I wanted to mislead him. It was more like I felt I needed to. I was trying to do as Danny had advised; make my banker more comfortable and ease his distress.

"Wow, Charlie. That sounds impressive. I mentioned that I had been hearing good things about your place. I have, and it wasn't from just one person. There have been three or four people who said flattering things at some of the chamber meetings and some others that I bumped into at various places. Now I'm beginnin' to understand why. I really like what I'm hearin'. "

"Thank you. I really appreciate that, and it excites me. We've been focusing on customer experiences, too. So it's nice to see that people have noticed. I've shifted some other personnel around, had one guy quit, promoted another, I mean besides Kevin, and so on and so forth. Anyway I came to the conclusion that while we're improving processes, our store culture needed to change, too."

Clancy nodded understanding. Then right when things were going well, out of the blue, he brought up the subject that I hoped had been lost in our conversation. "How are you doing with the budget you presented at the first of the year?" He leaned forward in anticipation.

I tried to camouflage my distress, but didn't feel that I was doing it very well. I reached for my brief case to pull out the budget reprint thinking it would give me time to think about an answer. I needed to stay confident. Then, I don't know where it came from, but I said, "You know, I've decided that I'm going to get some help with budgeting next year. Oh, by the way, here's a copy of the budget I gave you originally."

I passed it to him and then continued, "I don't think I benefit that much from a budget drawn from an accountant's perspective. That's numbers; addition and subtraction. My accountant handles those. But just like I mentioned that the employee productivity ratio seems to me to be always 'backward-looking,' my budgets have become that way as well. When I find that I missed it, it's over. I really don't have a way to tweak it or know what to do about it."

"I need ongoing experienced feedback from within the industry to see how the numbers work together, make projections and keep us focused on our goals. Ideally, they'd make suggestions if we fall short of the goals and give us suggestions as to how to recover and plot new directions. It seems to me that that would be much more beneficial and more helpful from an operational perspective."

I didn't know where all of that came from. I thought about continuing to lead the dance while shooting from the hip, but paused to let my last statements linger. I decided to react only after he responded. I didn't have to wait long.

"Do you have someone in mind who can help with that?"

"I've already put out some feelers, and I've heard about a couple guys," I said, and then concluded. "Yeah, I'm sure I'll come up with somebody."

He nodded again. This time I decided to redirect the conversation and see if it stuck. "The main thing, or at least the thing that I am so darned excited about is that we are making progress, good progress. It's tangible and it's moving pretty quickly. We've been having the best Saturday business that we've had for years ... maybe ever. I'm going to run some numbers and figure out if it would be a good idea to open on Saturday afternoons. If it pencils out, we can make some quick headway right there."

He nodded and, at that point, his body language told me he was satisfied.

"Well, keep me posted. I'll be anxious to hear how it's going. Call anytime if you have questions. It sounds like you're on a good path." He pushed his chair back, stood, and offered me his hand.

"Thanks, Clancy." I said, and then before he could respond, I added, (Are you ready for this?) "I'm going to document all of the processes we're working on so we can modify and tweak them. I'm starting to see another store or two in my future one day and having the processes documented will make it easier."

I was afraid he might laugh, or even worse, snort or scoff. But he didn't, he simply stated. "That's a good idea, Charley. It doesn't hurt to plan ahead. That's for sure."

Was I skipping or perhaps even walking on air as I left the bank? Maybe! It felt like it.

As I walked to the parking lot I began thinking about how I would have handled this meeting if we hadn't already begun our *Incremental Improvement Process*. The thought was scary. Before I even reached my truck, I pulled out my cell phone to call Danny.

As I opened the door, he answered. I climbed in and sat to talk.

"How'd it go, my man?" he asked.

"You know what?" I said.

"What?"

"I just grew a pair!"

I told him the entire story and he celebrated the success with me.

I wanted to get back to the store before closing, and he said someone was paging him, so I said, "I can't wait to get together again, so you can teach us more about the system."

"Well, I've been hungry for Mexican food, do you want to meet at the Bluffs next week? I'm buying."

"I'd love that, but you know the drill; you don't buy! You OK with me bringing Kevin again?" I asked.

"Sure, what night?"

"Wednesday, say 7:00?"

"Works for me, see you then."

***

When I walked back into the store, Kevin and Terrance were assisting customers at the registers. Several others were milling about. I liked the way it looked. We hadn't been this busy for quite a while. As I began helping them catch up, I saw Kevin glance nervously at me. I knew he was trying to assess how the meeting had gone. I smiled and gave him a "thumbs up" and he was visibly relieved. It was a nice flurry of business, but we soon caught up.

"Hey, Kevin, when you get a chance come back to my office, would you?" I said.

"Sure thing, boss, be there in a bit."

I checked my emails and voice mails. Nothing had gone off the rails.

"Knock-knock," Kevin said. He must have pretty much followed me to the back.

"Come on in. Sit down."

After he pulled up a chair I recounted the visit to the

bank. I shared with him the comments Clancy had made about the good things he'd been hearing around the community. Kevin was clearly excited.

"That's awesome! So he was OK, then?"

"Yeah, I've got to get a handle on budgeting, but I think the positive comments he'd been hearing went a long way to help."

Kevin nodded and then said, "We were really busy while you were gone, but it didn't seem like you were gone that long, so I didn't know how it went."

"No, I wasn't ... it was short and sweet. The meeting was at 2:30." I glanced and my watch and then continued, "It's only 4:15 now and I've been back for a little while."

"I didn't really expect you back today, at least not this early. But I'm glad you're here. I made a decision about store meetings and I hope you're alright with it. I've changed them to Friday mornings instead of Tuesdays. We don't have to pay anybody extra for coming in because only Jerry and Charlene aren't on the schedule since it's one of our busiest mornings. They pick up their checks on Friday mornings anyway, so we'll just tell them to pick them up at 7:45."

I nodded. "And they're OK with that?"

"Yeah, at the worst we have to pay them for 15 minutes. But they said they didn't mind coming in at that time. They'd rather do that than come in on days they weren't gonna be here."

"So when does this start?"

"Tomorrow morning, if that's OK."

"Sure," I said, "It's your call."

"Ok. Any chance you can join us tomorrow?"

"Yeah, I can be there. Anything you need from me?"

"Well, if you've been hearing good things about the store, it would be nice if you'd share that."

"No problem. I think that'd be good. Oh, by the way, what

does your Wednesday night look like next week?"
He shrugged his shoulders, "Nothing planned that I know of. Why?"
"I'm going to meet up with Danny at the Bluffs again. I'd love to have you there if you can make it."
"Sounds great. Mexican again?"
"Yep."
"Great. I love that place."

***

When I got home that evening, I quickly realized that I should have called Julie and brought her up to speed about my meeting at the bank. It had hurt her feelings that I didn't. It seems it had caused her to feel more anxious, too. That's the last thing she needed and the last thing I wanted to do.
"Ok, listen, I'm sorry. You're right. I should have called. I guess I was focused on getting back to the store." I hesitated, reading her body language and facial expression. She had her poker face on, so I eventually continued, "Come sit down with me and I'll tell you all about it."
I took her hand and headed to the kitchen table. I wanted to be looking at her while we were talking. I was already in the doghouse; no need to make things worse. After we sat down, she surprised me by speaking first.
"I've been worried sick all day, and then when you didn't call me, I started fearing the worst." She began to sniffle.
"Julie, please look at me. I understand. I'm sorry. It was inconsiderate of me not to call. It makes it seem like I was excluding you, but nothing could be further from the truth. I just got caught up in myself, and the things I needed to do."
She nodded, sniffled again and asked, "So, how did it go?"
"It went well, surprisingly well, actually."

I recounted the meeting and gloated over the fact that I had told Clancy that I was beginning to visualize additional stores. I celebrated the fact that he hadn't laughed in my face at the idea.

She nodded and then said, "You wouldn't, really, would you?"

"Wouldn't what?"

"Wouldn't want another store."

"Maybe. If I can prove to myself that I can make this one work and if we can get to the point that we're making some money, then yeah, maybe so."

She managed a small smile. I knew it was going to take a while for things to get back to normal at the ole home place, but at least the ice was beginning to melt.

I reached over, grabbed both of her hands in mine and tried to figure something romantically fitting for the moment. I had nothin', so I opted instead for "how about some Chinese?"

***

Kevin dropped by my office the following morning to let me know that the store meeting would start soon. I told him I would be with him momentarily. I needed to respond to an email from Clancy. It was a nice note thanking me for attending the meeting. He was complimentary, and it was a great way to start the morning.

I typed, "It was good to see you, too, Clancy. Thank you for your support and advice. I look forward to the next update." That wasn't entirely true, but I can honestly say that I was beginning to frame the relationship in a different light.

From the sales floor I heard Kevin tell everybody to huddle up. As I walked up to join them I heard him call the meeting to order.

"Good morning, everyone. Thank you for being here and being on time and all that stuff. How's everybody doing this morning?"

There were mostly positive responses

"By now, you have an idea what these meetings are about. We're working together to improve the performance of the store. The better we all understand what we're trying to accomplish the more likely we'll be able to do that. We're focusing on four things that can improve our profitability. Profitability is what allows us to get an occasional raise. Also Charley said that he is going to start offering some monthly or, at least, quarterly incentives if we make some goals that we're going to establish."

There were whoops and hollers around the service desk where everybody had gathered. Judging from facial expressions, the crew looked happy and genuinely engaged.

"Charley do you have anything more that you want to say about that?"

He caught me a little bit off guard. I stammered, "Well, nothing more on that, really. It's just as you said that, as a team, we have to improve performance and when we do, I want us all to benefit. Kevin mentioned four variables that we're going to be focusing on. If we can do that, improve those things, it'll be much better for all of us. Kevin will tell you more about what we're measuring and he'll probably share with you why we picked those four things. I'm sure it won't all happen today. These meetings are intended to be short, but they are going to be regular. Also, I want to say before I turn the meeting back over to Kevin that I've received some really good compliments about the store lately. Not the store itself really, but the way people have been treated here. I want to let you know that I am very proud of you and the changes we've made so far. I want us to become known as the friendliest store in town."

It was rewarding and exciting to see the smiles and the

positive body language from the team as I continued. "The one thing that will affect our ability to succeed more than anything else is what customers experience while they are shopping here. Make them feel welcome. Greet them with smiles and make them feel as if they're being greeted by good friends. If we do that, we've got a good start on what we need to accomplish."

I paused, looked around the room and then concluded, "That's about all I've got to say this morning. Other than, if you have suggestions about how we can do something better, please let Kevin or me know. Perhaps I've made myself somewhat unapproachable before. I didn't intend to, but that was brought up in some feedback I got the other day. Please know that my door is always open. I consider you a teammate." I turned toward him and said, "Kevin, that's all I've got."

He took my place in the center of the group and said, "Thanks, boss."

I decided to let him finish the meeting alone. I heard him continue as I walked away, "One of the things we have begun to measure is a number called conversion rate. We've placed traffic or customer counters at both of the doors that go outside. Maybe you saw Charley and I installing them ..."

Stores on Fire

Chapter 20

Wednesday evening, Kevin and I pulled out of the parking lot a little after 5:30. We were running a bit late so I called Danny from the road to let him know. He told me to make sure we brought the asset group management charts we had completed. I explained that we were already on our way, but when I mentioned it to Kevin, he said he had them and I was glad to hear it.

"Yeah, I brought the charts and all of the other notes that I've been taking, too. I've also written out some questions that were on my mind."

"What kind of questions?" I asked.

"Well, it's just things regarding pushing for improvement. How do we improve our customer count? How do we improve conversion rate? etc. But, now that I read them out loud, they sound kind of silly because they're just restating the goals in question form."

"I get that, but I don't think they're silly. If he gives us some more clues I'm sure we'll be able to take it from there. Remember he got us started thinking about consolidating vendors and the quantities we were buying and stuff like that. We responded and our margin is beginning to improve. Something has helped, anyway. It's been creeping up."

He thought for a moment and then replied. "I noticed that, too, and I suppose the vendor consolidation could be part of the reason, but you know what else has changed?"

I glanced at him, shrugged my shoulders, shook my head and waited.

"Walk-in traffic. We've got the counters up now and I would bet that when we check them the next time and compare them against our starting numbers they'll be higher. It really feels like we've been having more customers."

"Could be, but I don't see why increased traffic would improve our margin."

He smiled, wily like a fox. "Well, inside sales have higher margins. If we have more store traffic and that produces increased inside sales, then we produce margins more like a hardware store and less like a lumber yard. So, if inside traffic increases, then margin is likely to go up as well. Don't you think?"

I thought about it for a moment and knew that the reasoning was sound. "I guess so, although I hadn't thought about it. But, it makes me realize now that another benefit would be that we would produce a higher percentage of cash sales. That definitely would help improve cash flow."

Kevin nodded. "Boss, you didn't say how often you wanted the traffic counters read and recorded."

"No, we didn't talk about that, did we? I really don't know, but it seems that it wouldn't be a big problem to read and record them daily. Maybe start a spreadsheet so that we can start doing some comparisons. Sherry could help you put that together."

"You're right. It wouldn't take a whole lot of time, and it would definitely be interesting to monitor our progress. You know what though? I've been learning about spreadsheets at night. I've learned a lot, and it would be a good exercise for me to try my hand at something useful. If you don't mind, I'd like to try to write them myself and then, if I get stumped, I'll ask Sherry for her help. Would that be OK?"

"Sure. If you think you can do it, knock yourself out. That way, you can design it the way you want it. As I think about it, it will be interesting to compare this week to last week, but it would be more enlightening to compare it to the same time period. Once we have data for an entire year we can compare July 1st to July 1st, for example."

Kevin appeared to be chewing on what I had just said and then finally replied, "It seems to me it might be better to compare the first Monday of July regardless of date to the first Monday of July the previous year. The dates would move, the days wouldn't."

I got what he meant immediately. "You're right. Do you think you can make a spreadsheet that will do that?"

"I'll try. It doesn't sound too hard. I'll start working on it. In the meantime, I'll have someone start recording the numbers from the counters each day."

We rode quietly for a few miles. I remembered I hadn't asked for a while, "So, how's Rhonda doing? Is she getting excited about the baby?"

Kevin chuckled, "Yeah, she's getting excited alright. She's driving me absolutely nuts. She's been working on the nursery and everything. You saw that I bought some paint the other day didn't you?"

"Yeah, was that for the nursery?"

"Yes. That's what I worked on all last weekend. I'm going to give it another coat this weekend?"

"Thought that paint was supposed to be one coat."

"I'm sure it would have been if we wouldn't have been going over that crazy canary yellow that someone painted in there before we bought the house. It was god-awful, but the new color is going to look good, and Rhonda really likes it."

"That's what's important, right? I mean that Rhonda likes it."

Kevin laughed. "Yeah, you got that right. For me, I would have been fine putting up some nice bright pink curtains with that yellow and it would have looked just fine."

"No, you wouldn't."

He laughed again. "Well, maybe not, but she's the one we've got to please anyway, you know?"

"Oh, I know all about that, believe me. Have you been

working on names?"

"Oh, man don't even go there. We have books with baby names strung in all corners of the house, and you wouldn't believe how crazy some of them are."

I laughed and said, "Well, you know, I think Charley is a great name."

This time Kevin snorted and nearly choked on the iced tea he was drinking. When he regained his composure he said, "Oh, my lord. I don't think the world could handle another one. Besides, what if it's a girl?"

"Well, is it?"

"Can't say. Rhonda says we've got to have a reveal party. That's the big thing now, you know?"

"What the heck is a reveal party?"

"I guess you have a party and then at some point you do something clever to reveal whether the baby is a boy or a girl."

"Ok, gotcha. But you guys know, right?"

"Yeah, we know."

"Well, give me a little clue, maybe I can guess." I smiled.

"It's nunya."

"Nunya?" What do you mean?

"It's nunya business." This time Kevin nearly choked to death reveling in his own cleverness.

***

I glanced at the clock as we pulled into the parking lot. We had made really good time, and as it turned out, we arrived only a couple minutes late. The parking lot was not full, but there was a descent crowd.

"I don't think we'll have any problem finding a place to sit," I said.

I glanced around, but didn't see Danny's truck. Then, as if on cue, he pulled in and took the spot next to Clifford, the big red truck.

"Hey guys, how you doing?" He climbed out wearing jeans, a red plaid shirt, and his standard big smile.

"Hey Dan," said Kevin, "We're doing great. How about you?"

"Doing fine, Kevin. I'm looking forward to visiting with you guys."

After a round of handshakes, as we walked to the entrance, I joined the conversation. "We're looking forward to the evening, too, Danny. How was your drive up?"

We continued small talk while we waited for the hostess. When she arrived we requested a quiet area and a few moments later she seated us at the same table we had sat at the last time.

"This seems like deja vu all over again," Kevin joked.

Danny chuckled and said, "Man I'm surprised you remember anything, as much ground as we covered last time."

"Yeah, we went around the horn alright, but surprisingly enough, I think a lot of it stuck." Kevin smiled.

The waitress greeted us quickly and we ordered drinks, chips and guacamole.

"So," said Danny, "looks like you survived your trip to the bank."

"Yeah, I did, but I've got some work to do before the next one, or I'll be in trouble."

Danny shot a puzzled look. "What kind of work? What do you mean?"

"The meeting was progressing nicely. It seemed that things were going pretty well until he asked me how I was doing with the budget. I didn't have solid answers so I kind of bluffed my way through it. I don't want to do that anymore, so I'll need to figure out a way to get a handle on it before next time."

"When's the next time?"

I shrugged my shoulders. "Don't know for sure, but I'm guessing 90 days or something like that."

"That shouldn't be a problem. Have you ever heard about the Profit Explorer?"

"You're not talking about Ponce de Leon, are you?"

"Very funny, man," Danny said, as our drinks arrived.

Kevin drank first. "Oh! My that's good."

"I'm sorry I interrupted you, Danny. What is the Profit Explorer?" I asked.

"It's a program that I use to establish my budget and to help me stay on track. It takes a lot of the stress out of the process and it makes it all pretty easy. Really, it's more of a service than a program. It costs a little to be enrolled but they provide some coaching at the same time, so it's been a great investment for me."

"I want to learn more about it. It's kind of funny that you mention it; it kind of sounds like what I described to the banker. I'll give you a call sometime and get the details, but for tonight, I'd like to keep moving forward with the Incremental Improvement system, if that's OK."

"Gotcha," Danny said. "So where are you with the process?"

Kevin and I reviewed the cuts we'd made with some vendors and the other steps we had taken in reaction to his coaching and in keeping with the system. When we told him that our margin was improving it seemed to match his expectations.

"That doesn't surprise me. Especially since you're seeing more walk-in traffic. That's awesome. I think you're on the right track, don't you?"

"Sure feels like it," I said as Kevin nodded in agreement. "But we've got a long way to go."

Danny tilted his head, shrugged his shoulders and said, "Sure, but remember, it's an ongoing process and a push for continuous improvement. In other words, it's a path, not a destination."

I reached for my water, took a drink, smiled and said, "Well, that's a little disappointing."

"Didn't know what you signed up for, did you kid?" he smirked.

"I'm joking," I said. "Actually we're enjoying the ride."

"The farther you get into the process, the more you'll like it. The small improvements that you're seeing now will start snowballing and eventually make real differences."

Kevin nodded and then joined the conversation, "What should our next steps be?"

"Well, do you have the asset group and critical keys chart with you?"

"Yep," Kevin said as he fumbled through his note book.

"Here it is." He laid the chart on the table.

Danny began pointing as he talked. "Ok, the last time we were together we talked about the first two Critical Keys in the Products asset group; 'Buy Them' and 'Process Them.' One thing I want to make sure you understand is that the Opportunity Check Points we discussed were not a comprehensive list. They were just supposed to get you started."

Kevin said, "Yeah, we get that, and just so you'll know, we took the 'Process Them' Critical Key further and identified some additional opportunities for improvement there."

I jumped in to help, "Yeah, we noticed that we had some real bottlenecks moving freight inside the store. When we moved paint to the sales floor, for example, it was much more difficult and took more time than it should have. The pallet jack was hard to maneuver around all the constrictions and, in the past, we had damaged some things. You know what it's like to clean up paint when it spills. Well, anyway, we found that by moving some counters a little we could make the process easier and a lot faster, and we know it will save us some mark downs."

The waitress arrived and took our dinner orders.

After she walked away, Danny reconvened the discussion. "That's really good about you finding efficiency improvements. As you said it'll make you money a couple different ways: improve payroll productivity and improve margin if it decreases mark-downs. Charley, do you remember noticing that all of the gondolas in my store run the same direction?"

I nodded.

"That's not an accident. When they designed my store they suggested that we do that for efficiency and it's made a big difference. And, in addition to the point you made about moving freight with less hassle, it also requires fewer employees to staff the store because you can see down the aisles the full length of the store. Therefore, each team member can handle a bigger area. You know, at some point in time, you need to consider rearranging your store, too. It'd give it new life and really give you a boost. I'll hook you up with my designers if you like the way my store looks."

"Yeah, OK. Someday maybe. You know the main thing I remember about your store's layout is the angled aisles. I thought that was really cool," I said.

"I like it, too. It seems to me that it makes the store more interesting and certainly makes it different than most. It's important to differentiate your store. Heck, here we are, you're in the business and even you are talking about unique it is."

"I'm trying to visualize how you have angled aisles if all of the gondolas are running the same direction?" Kevin asked.

"The gondolas have different terminal points, in other words, they're not all the same length. We marked the aisles with tape to emphasize the angles and make sure that the employees don't interrupt the visuals that we

created."
"I still don't get it," Kevin said.
Danny pulled a napkin and began to sketch.

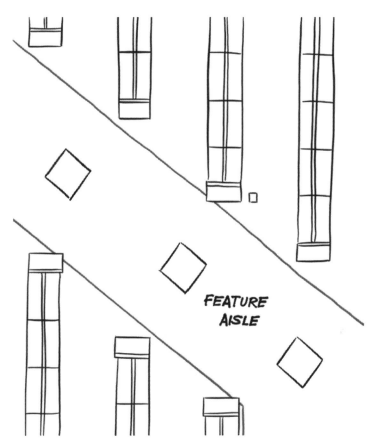

FEATURE
AISLE

Kevin watched closely and then after a few moments said, "Oh, OK, now I see. I thought the gondolas were at angles." "No, that would chew up sales space. The designers told me that by doing it this way it would still be efficient and help guide customers through the entirety of the store. They were right. It definitely helped sales and customers really seem to like it."

Dinner arrived, sizzling and smelling good enough to eat. "Can I get you anything else?" The waitress asked.

We all glanced at each other with goofy looks until Danny responded, "Looks like we're good. You might bring us some more chips sometime, but don't make a special trip ... just whenever you're back this way."

She said that she would. Funny how good food can slow down conversation, but it always does. We enjoyed a great meal. The waitress stopped back by to check on us, bring the chips, and ask if we'd like more drinks, but we all declined. I said that she could bring me the check whenever she was ready.

We told Danny about a couple other things we had changed to help improve efficiencies with processing and transporting freight. He gave us a few more suggestions and then brought up the next critical key.

"Now," he said, "when you get to the 'Price Them' critical key, well, that gets a little more challenging. First thing you need to know is that we're not talking about how you attach a price to an item, although we did discuss that, and based on that discussion, you're not pricing individual items anymore, right?"

We answered in unison, nodding our heads together, "Right."

Danny continued, "Pricing is more about deciding and implementing a strategy. Then, probably the most important part ... communicating your prices."

Kevin spoke up, "What do you mean by pricing strategy? Better yet, what is your pricing strategy?"

"Mine? It varies from department to department."

We sat there not knowing what to ask, so he soon continued. "There are basically three pricing strategies: 1. Price-leader, 2. Competitive and 3. Prestige pricing. Here's what I mean by each. Price-leader strategy is exactly what the name implies. On any given item your plan is to be the lowest price in the market."

"That sounds impossible, or at the very least, dangerous," I said.

Danny held up a hand, "Hold on, hoss; Let me explain what the other strategies are before you get too excited, and then I'll tell you how I use price-leading as part of my overall strategy."

I nodded.

"A competitive pricing strategy is kind of self-explanatory, too, except there is a caveat. The main focus has to be *maintaining competitive pricing with stores that are slotted the same as yours.*"

"I have no idea what you're talking about," said Kevin. "Slotted the same?"

"Oh, that's from the Discovery-Based Retail book, isn't it?" I asked.

Danny nodded. "Did you read it?"

I acknowledged that I had.

Danny chuckled and said, "Sounds like you better share your copy with Kevin, or get him one of his own."

"Well, somebody explain it to me for heaven's sake cause I'm not following the conversation."

Danny continued. "OK, your store competes against other stores, but not every one of those stores operates within the same slot. For example, there are stores that compete with you that are slotted as convenience stores. They're usually smaller stores. They are quicker to get in and out of. You can usually park right out front, grab a couple things and be on your way in a jiff. They often have pretty good locations, but because of their size they have less inventory. The main reason they appeal to people is, as the name implies, convenience ... convenience in time and location. The key here is that their prices are usually higher and they need to be. They don't have the volume that other store types generate. Their average sale is smaller, too, because of the same reasons."

He took a drink before continuing, "Your store, I'm guessing would be slotted as what is called a 'regional competitor.' Regional competitor stores are usually bigger, have more items, deeper inventories and therefore, more to choose from. Like I said, convenience stores appeal primarily for convenience where regional competitor stores must be more price-focused. Regional competitors get bigger jobs because of their additional inventories, but they're not selling simply because of convenience. They possess other attributes that create draw. I mentioned I thought that's the slot your store would operate in, because that's how my store is slotted, too."

"I don't know," I said. "If you were operating in our market you would kick our butts."

Danny shrugged, "Maybe so; probably so. But, that just shows that you've got a lot of work to do to get to where you want to be."

"So, a store is either a convenience store or a regional competitor? Is that right?"

"No, there are actually 3 other store slot types, but we'll just talk about one more of them because I want to keep our conversation moving forward. You can borrow Charley's book and read about the others. It really is an interesting concept."

"OK, already. I'll order one for him," I said.

They both smiled and Danny shrugged his shoulders and said, "Solid investment, my friend."

"OK," said Kevin. "What's the other one you're going to tell me about?"

"Destination stores. They are the biggest stores in the market; think big-box store or similar. They are usually much bigger than regional competitors. They have larger inventories, larger in-store selections. They're often perceived to have the best prices, but usually don't really beat regional competitors by much, if at all. But in this case, perception is our enemy."

"I know what you're talking about. Some people who complain about our pricing say they can buy the stuff much cheaper at the Builders' Market. I know it's not true, but I don't want to get into arguments with them," Kevin said.

"That's what I'm talking about. Perceptions. We'll talk about that in a moment, but let me finish."

Kevin nodded.

"So when you undertake a competitive pricing strategy it requires some recon. You have to know where you stand. But the important thing is to compare against the stores slotted the same as yours. If you compare yourselves against convenience stores you may feel good, but it won't give you accurate information. The thing is, you want to capture some of your competitors' business, but it will likely have to come from stores that are slotted the same as yours. If people like the warehouse destination store environment, they'll probably be hard to redirect. If they're drawn by the convenience factors a store offers, you may not be able to match those. But, competitors slotted the same, now that's a different story. You'll have the most in common with those stores. There's a good chance you'll appeal to their customers because your store will be similar to theirs. You can win those battles. Set your sights there first."

"OK. I get that. That's how you set up a competitive pricing strategy," said Kevin. "But, you mentioned prestige pricing. I don't know what that is either. And, then, you said you use all of the pricing strategies. How's that possible?"

"OK. For example, I sell a lot of grills at my store. Grills and accessories. You saw my grill department didn't you, Charley?"

I nodded. "Very impressive."

"Some of the brands have MAPP, you know, minimum advertised pricing policies. But the ones that don't, I make sure no one, and I mean no one sells them cheaper. I do the same thing with the propane, wood chips, sauces, dry rubs, accessories ... all of that related stuff. I am definitely the price leader there. So, in that one department I use a 'price-leader' approach."

"Doesn't your margin suck?" I asked.

"In that department, yeah, it's not the best. But what it does for traffic and perception and visibility around town, well, that's priceless. We have literally become the 'go to' location for outdoor cooking and accessories. We're establishing price image by leveraging one department without giving margin away everywhere else."

"Can I get you anything more?" the waitress asked.

I glanced at my watch, "You guys are probably thinking about closing up, aren't you?"

She nodded and smiled. "Soon, but take your time. We'll be cleaning up for a while."

"OK, thanks. Here' my credit card."

Danny watched her walk away and then continued. "So in most of my other departments, I use a competitive pricing strategy. But in my cabinet sales area, I use a prestige pricing approach."

Kevin was paying close attention. "So, what's that and how do you do it?"

"You saw my cabinet display area, didn't you Charley?"

I nodded. "Oh, I saw it alright. That had to have set you back a few bucks."

Danny smiled and nodded. "Yeah, it was an investment. That's for sure. But, then again vendors helped out quite a bit. When they saw what I had planned they competed to make sure they were part of it, and I think most of them think it's been a pretty good investment from their perspective. But anyway, where I'm going with this is that people can't have a cabinet buying experience like we offer anywhere around us. So are my cabinet prices higher? Yes, they probably are. But in that one department my customers are paying for our efforts to expose them to the latest trends and to the best consultation available for miles around. We switch the displays out regularly to make sure we're always offering the same finishes and features they're currently seeing on HGTV. We offer premium brands in an upscale environment and they are willing to pay for the experience."

"Seems like you would miss out on all the people that want to replace cabinets in apartments and rental houses," Kevin said.

Danny shrugged his shoulders. "Yeah, maybe, but with the cabinets I do sell I make good money and people love to just hang out in that area of the store. It's an experience."

"Kevin, think about what our cabinet area looks like," I said.

"I walked through your cabinet department when I came up to your store," Danny offered. "It looks pretty tired. If someone wanted to replace a kitchen they wouldn't be inspired by what you're showing."

I nodded and suddenly felt a little overwhelmed.

I think that Danny read my body language. "Remember, hoss, it's a process. Take one bite at a time. You'll get there."

Stores on Fire

Chapter 21

"You seem kind of quiet," Kevin said.

I glanced at him, smiled and said, "Do I? I guess, I'm just thinking about everything we talked about tonight. We've got a long way to go, don't we?"

"Yeah, boss. We do. But the most important thing is that at least we're on our way now. It seems like we didn't even have a direction before, and now we do, so I'm stoked. You need to stay that way, too."

I thought about it for a moment. "You're right, and, I am, but it seems a little daunting."

"Yeah, but daunting and undoable are two different things."

I nodded as my cellphone rang. Caller ID showed it was Danny. I put him on the truck speaker.

"Hey Danny."

"Hey, you know what I was thinking?" Danny asked.

"Nope."

"Why don't you guys make a trip down to my store one of these weekends. I'd like to show Kevin around so when we talk about things he'll understand where we're coming from. It'd be good for him to see the store layout and kitchen department we talked about tonight."

I glanced over at Kevin. He was smiling and nodding.

"Think we have a big 10-4 there buddy. Looks like Kevin is in. When were you thinking?"

"Well this weekend's out, but I'm pretty much open after that."

"OK, sounds good. Listen we'll talk about it, and I'll give you a call tomorrow or Friday. Would that work?"

"Sure, sounds good. Just let me know. It's a bit of a drive, so you guys ought to bring your wives, spend a night and have a little get-a-away."

"OK. Well, we'll talk about that. Thanks again for the help tonight and for all the other times, too."

"Your welcome! Sure. Anyway just let me know when you can make it."

"Will do, talk to you later."

I pressed the 'end call' button, smiled at Kevin and said, "Sounds like fun, doesn't it? The yard can pick up the travel and lodging expenses, and we'll write it off as training."

"Sounds awesome, boss. It's been a while since Rhonda and I've gotten away, so I know she'll be excited, too."

"It'll be nice for her and Julie to get to know each other better. I know Julie's mentioned wanting to do that. Maybe, they can go shopping or something."

"Well, unless the yard is picking those expenses as well, I'm not too excited about that part." He laughed but I could tell he was enthused about the trip.

***

The following day I arrived at the store early and was surprised to see Kevin already there.

"You beat me again," I said. "How long have you been here?"

Kevin glanced at his watch and shrugged his shoulders. "I don't know, 30 minutes or so maybe."

"So what are you working on?"

"I was going over the spread sheet I made to track customer counts. We don't have anything to compare to except the previous couple weeks, but we had 13 percent more people this week than last and 10 percent more last week than the week before. Remember I told you that I thought it was busier?"

I nodded my head. "Yes, but there will be fluctuations

from week to week. I guess we can't read too much in to a few weeks, but that's why it's important for us to keep the journal. Still, it is encouraging, isn't it?"

"Oh, yeah. It definitely is, boss. Remember when we used that online-calculator to help us set our goals? We used a two person per day average increase in traffic. I think as slow as things were around here that we're going to beat that by a bunch."

"Maybe, but like I said, don't read too much into a good couple of weeks."

"It's more than that," Kevin said. "Don't you feel the change? Don't you see it? Don't you just know that we're on the right track?"

I smiled. "Yeah, I do. I'm just trying to guard about being too optimistic. But, oh well, what the heck? I think we can blow our goal numbers away, too."

Kevin cupped his hands to his mouth to do his best "carnival barker" voice. "Attention shoppers and all other interested parties! The big man is back on board. Stand back. I think he's gonna blast off ... the sky is now the limit."

We both laughed. It was fun to be enthusiastic and to share visions of success. It felt really good to know that Kevin was fully on board, had taken ownership and that I wasn't slaying the dragon by myself.

***

Over the next several weeks we continued to work with more of the Critical Keys, locating opportunities and making changes. We were definitely making headway by then and we knew it. Customer count, conversion rate, and margin began to climb and none of it was accidental. Transaction size had not increased like the other three variables, so we decided to focus on that. Like Danny had predicted would happen, as we began gaining momentum, we were anxious to make more positive changes. Kevin and my relationship grew, and I learned that, in many regards, I could trust his judgements as much or more than I could my own. We made the trip to Danny's store down in Freemont and had a great time. Kevin enjoyed seeing what time (and money) could do for improving a store. He came home even more fired up having seen how Danny's three-level pricing strategy looked in practice.

Rhonda and Julie hit it off and were becoming good friends. As they began spending more time together Julie seemed to return more to the way she was before her parents' accident. I'm not sure it was specifically because of her new friendship. In fact, I'm sure it wasn't. Time, as they say, is the great healer, but having a new good friend didn't hurt either. Julie enjoyed hanging out with Rhonda and she told me that she thought that she and Rhonda were a lot alike. She liked helping Rhonda make preparations for the new arrival, too. That worried me a little bit. I didn't want Julie to get any funny ideas.

One night Kevin and Rhonda invited family and friends over for a cookout. It was "nothing special" they said, but when some of the ladies began to notice the blue drinks being served to everyone, some of them caught on. I, like most of the other men, was oblivious. To me and my male counterparts they were just blue drinks, not some secret coded message. As long as they had tequila in them, we guys were all good. The ladies had to explain to us what it meant.

The next day when Kevin came in to my office for our now regular meetings I spoke first. "Charles. Charley. The little Charlooney. It has a nice ring to it, doesn't it?" I didn't look up.

Kevin laughed and said, "Rings just fine for you I guess,

but I'm leaning toward Kevin Jr."

"Really? That's awesome, Kevin."

Kevin chuckled again and replied, "I said I'm leaning toward it, but Rhonda said not to lean too hard or I'll fall over. Nah, I think she's got several names on the list, but I don't think KJ is one of them."

We exchanged more small talk and additional jabs before getting to work.

"You said that you wanted to talk about the progress we were making on increasing transaction size, boss." He paused and then added, "or the lack of it."

"Yeah, I thought we should look at it. It seems that the other variables of the system are going up pretty good, but not transaction size."

"I noticed that too, so I thought after we discuss it this morning I'll share our ideas in the Friday morning store meeting. Oh, by the way, those have been going real well. Everybody is participating now and I think they look forward to them. They are beginning to see themselves as a team, and they're acting more like one, too."

"Awesome. You've done a really good job with those meetings, by the way."

"Thanks, boss. I was a little uncomfortable with them the first few weeks, but now they kind of seem old hat."

I nodded my head. "So, have you put any ideas together on increasing transaction size?"

Kevin pulled his notebook and started fumbling through the pages. "Yeah, I've been doing a lot of reading. I really enjoyed that book you gave me, by the way, so thanks again. I've read that and a couple others and have had some ideas of my own. So, anyway, yeah, I've got some ideas."

"Let me hear what you're thinking," I said.

"OK. Here goes. Here's my main premise: transaction size will only go up as a result of improved sales processes."

I rubbed my chin and must have looked perplexed.

He continued as if to clarify. "That's the only way they can increase. But's here's the thing; Sales processes can be either active or passive."

"What do you mean?"

"Well, if I'm helping a customer with paint, for example, I can suggest a particular brush ... a better brush. So, if the customer bought the better brush I suggested, it would drive the transaction size up, right?" He didn't pause long enough for me to answer. "That's an active process. I have to be there and be *actively* involved in an exchange which will increase the transaction size."

I nodded. "Yeah. Ok. I get that."

"But, what if I'm not there? What if I'm waiting on someone else?"

"We miss an opportunity?"

"Yeah, we do. But the thing is that we can't be assured that we'll have a clerk helping everyone who's buying paint. And maybe paint isn't the best example, but you get what I mean."

I nodded, still wondering where he was going.

"But, if we have signs near the paint spelling out the same thing, it won't be exactly the same but it would be better than no sales process at all. That would be a passive sales process. And, just like the basis of the incremental improvement system if we put those signs up once, they would keep working for us until we changed them."

"So you're talking about POP, 'point-of-purchase' information?"

"No. Not really. POP is informational for sure. And it can help in choosing between two products or brands. But what I'm visualizing is recommending *specific* products as add-ons at the shelf just like a salesperson would do. We'd have to have them printed. I don't want them to look junky. They would need to be branded and specific, and I suppose they could be overdone, but they would serve as passive sales aids. So, I guess they wouldn't be POP they would be APRs."

"APR?"

"Yeah, Associated Product Recommendations. Heck we could even market APRs as an advantage of shopping here. Something like: 'Watch for our APR tags throughout the store. These tags indicate ways to make your job easier, faster, cleaner or more cost effective.'"

I didn't have to think about it too long. "I like it. That's a great idea. We could make all of the tags the same color so they'd be easy to spot. And, you know what? I think we can program our computer system to suggest things for the checkers to recommend based upon a customer purchases, too."

"Yeah, I believe you're right. I think I read that somewhere in the manual. The downside of that is that the customer has already left the department by then and is focused on leaving. But still, it's probably a good idea."

He paused as I nodded, but then continued shortly. "The other thing I was thinking about that kind of goes along with that is we could buy some televisions, use them as digital monitors, and hang them strategically around the store. You know ... where people are lingering for a while. We could put one where they're waiting for their paint to shake, or over there where they're waiting at the tool rental area. We would make messages to display and figure out how to loop them. We could tell about services we offer, specials we have going, special events. Heck, we could even thank veterans for their service to help strengthen our community connection. Congratulate the football and debate teams and stuff like that. I checked and the cost for big TVs have fallen dramatically. I think we could get it all going pretty much on the cheap."

I rubbed my chin while I thought about it. I remembered

seeing monitors in many of the big stores which were doing basically the same thing. Why not our store, I thought, before asking, "Who would make the messages?"

"We have several people working here that I think would do great, maybe even some of the part-timers, but I know that Terrance makes videos as a hobby. He would already have the software that it would take, and I'll bet he could do them without any problem."

I nodded my head. "Get me some firm figures and we'll take another look at it, but I think it's a great idea."

I was already blown away by what Kevin had brought to the meeting, but I could tell he wasn't done. "What else do you have?"

"OK, well, all of these ideas came from thinking about the products asset group and from the opportunity check points we made from the 'Display them' and 'Sell them' critical keys."

I nodded.

"I think that we should set up a queue checkout system like Danny had in his store. Remember he had a single aisle leading to his registers. Customers waited at the end for the next available person to check them out. They had lined both sides of the waiting area with impulse items, remember that?"

"Yeah. He said the designers suggested that for his new store layout when they worked with him."

"Yeah. I know. I watched people go through there the Saturday morning we were there. They picked up a lot of different items. It looked like all the things they had merchandised there would produce good margins, too. I think that was by design, so I'm guessing Danny had it planned that way. Anyway, so that would be another passive sales technique. Get items to where people are going to be exposed to them. A queue checkout system is perfect for that, and from what I've read, most customers prefer them, too. You know it pisses a lot of people off if they choose a checkout line at a store and its goes slower than all the others. And with our increase in traffic I think the timing is right."

"Yeah, I like what Danny did in his store, and if we ever have our store redesigned, we'll probably do it as well."

Kevin nodded, but looked disappointed.

The phone rang. Speak of the devil. Danny was on the line so I put him on speaker.

"Hey, Danny. How's it going?" I asked. "Kevin and I are sitting here developing some strategies."

"That's good son, that's good. What have you come up with?"

I told him about Kevin's ideas for APRs and the monitors.

"Man, I like that. I'm gonna get my people working on that this afternoon, too. That's awesome."

I glanced at Kevin and his head appeared to be inflated like a smiling balloon.

"What else did you come up with?" Danny asked. "Maybe I can steal some more ideas."

"Well, that's about as far as we've gotten for now. Kevin mentioned he'd like to make a queue checkout like you have, but I told him we'd have to wait on that until we redesign the sales floor."

Danny didn't respond for a moment but then finally answered. "Well, that's about the stupidest thing I've ever heard."

I was shocked. "Why? Isn't the queue system working for you?"

"Damn straight. It works great. Didn't mean to sound like a poet there. But, why would you wait on doing something that could help your business, today? Increase your sales, today? Improve your margin, today? I don't get it."

I was defenseless. There was no good answer so I pulled an excuse instead. "I just don't think we have the room."

"That's BS, and you know it. You guys could figure out a way to move a few things around and make it happen."

I knew he was right. I had defaulted to my old way of approaching things ... **seeing barriers instead of opportunities**. "OK. OK. You guys win. We'll figure out a way to do it. We won't wait."

"You know, the more things you do to improve business now, the quicker you can see your way to remodeling and making the other changes you want, right?"

Kevin was smiling. Why were these two men conspiring against me?

My answer was short. "Yes."

Danny left it there and I was glad he did. "Hey, the reason I'm calling is remember when I told you about the Profit Explorer. It's that budgeting and goal setting service I use. Would you like to talk to them and learn more about it? I think it would be a good move for you."

I had almost forgotten about it, and I thought, man I am lucky that Clancy hasn't called again. "I wouldn't mind hearing about it. Seeing how it works and checking out the cost."

"Would it be alright if I have them give you a call?" Danny asked.

"Yeah. That'd be fine."

"OK. I'll do it. Expect a call from a guy named Gary."

"Gary?"

"Yep."

"OK, gotcha. So, what else is going on?" I asked.

"That's about it, son."

"Wait a minute, Danny. Do you have a couple more minutes?"

"Yeah, a few."

"Great. What things have you guys done to improve transaction size?"

His answer was quick. "Well, in addition to the queue

check system we also make sure to use every opportunity
to put impulse items in front of our customers."

"You mean on the counters at the register?"

"No, not really, I don't like them there so much. They slow
down the checkout process and make the counters look
junky. I think if you get messy there it creates security
issues. Nah, I'm talking about using wing displays on the
end caps, clip strips in every aisle, floor stacks where
they're appropriate ... those kinds of things. Also, I have
trained my staff to always have an associated item
featured on any end cap we build. All those things pay big
dividends in add-on sales and margin, too. When you can
increase two of the variables of the Incremental
Improvement Equation at one time you really notice it."

Kevin was writing feverishly.

Danny continued. "But I think that we made the biggest
gains on transaction size when we started working with
the staff. We made sure they understood what we were
trying to accomplish and why. After they bought in to the
why and the what for, then it was a matter of coaching
them to be better sales people."

"Tell me more about that, Danny," Kevin said.

"Well, you know, sometimes our staff showed the cheapest
items we had. And I mean things all the way from windows
to power tools, and from shower enclosures to paint. It
didn't matter what it was, I noticed they always showed
the cheapest thing we had. Many times they didn't even
tell customers about the better items and why they were
worth the price difference. You can increase transaction
size by selling more items in the transaction like you guys
were planning, but sometimes it's just as easy or maybe
even easier to sell them more expensive items. If customers
understand why the price is higher on one item versus
another, often they'll decide they want the features of the
better item. In their minds, or in your mind, or in my mind,

anyone's mind, once value exceeds price, we buy. That's the way it's always been and probably the way it will always be. So the secret to selling higher priced items is to increase the perception of value. It won't cause everybody to go with the higher priced item every time, but many times it will. Cha-ching. The transaction size goes up."

"I think that we have some people working here who are scared to try to recommend the better, more expensive, products," Kevin said.

"I did too, hoss. I did too. Some personalities and some people are just made that way."

"So how did you handle that?"

"Well, that's a matter of understanding the personalities of your staff. Some of the ones who had an aversion to selling had great interest, aptitudes and skills for just "helping" people. So it was matter of training that group of people to understand that they were helping people and not so much selling to them. I had personality testing done with my staff. That was helpful for a number of reasons. Once I learned what made 'em tick, it was easier to bring them along, build a better team and that kind of stuff. You know, different strokes for different folks."

"So where did you get that done?" I asked.

"Give the NRHA a call; they can help you with that. Hey, listen guys. I've got to go. I've got an appointment with a contractor in about 10 minutes. Charley, I'll tell the Profit Explorer guy to give you a call."

"OK, great. Thanks for the help, Danny."

"See you, Danny," Kevin said.

After the phone conversation was over I looked sheepishly at Kevin and said. "OK, make some sketches of the current cash wrap and start thinking of some ideas to make a queue."

"You got it, boss."

Chapter 22

Over the next few weeks we planned a queue checkout system and ordered some short gondolas to put our ideas in place. We decided to pull items from various departments to stock the counters that lined the waiting aisle. We did that instead of setting up reorder numbers at both locations. We thought it would save us some inventory duplication and allow us to switch out the items more frequently. We selected high margin items that we thought customers would likely buy if they saw them. Our goal was to increase transaction size. But if, as Danny had suggested, we could kill two birds with one stone (My apologies to the Audubon society) and also raise margin a little bit, so much the better. To say the least, it didn't work flawlessly at first. And of course, we had some customers gripe about the whole thing. But truthfully can you change anything in your store without hearing some complaints? It seemed to cause a lot of confusion until we bought some signs to help direct customers to where we wanted them to go. We also put little adhesive vinyl footprints on the floor leading the way. That may have helped, too. Anyway, they looked cute. People have adjusted to the change now and it's working well. We frequently restock the area so I know it's producing additional sales. We've even added a few high-margin items there now that we don't stock anywhere else in the store.

We bought televisions like Kevin suggested. (He prefers that we call them flat-screen monitors.) We explored investing in digital players for them, but didn't pull the trigger. We may revisit that and buy them sometime, but to save a few bucks we started with a single DVD player.

We ran cables from the player to a splitter and then cables from the splitter to all of the TVs. That meant they all played the same messages, which wasn't ideal, but it allowed us a lower entry point. We placed them in three locations and, as I recall, even though we went with bigger TVs, I think they were 58", we only had a little over a grand in the whole shootin' match. To tell you the truth I didn't know if they helped at all until one day one of our regular customers approached me and said, "Hey, I saw on one of your TVs there that you can put shingles on the roof now? Is that right?"

"Yeah," I said. "We've been doing that for two or three years."

He looked exasperated. "Well, doggone it. I'm sorry. I didn't know you guys did that. I bought shingles from Samson Lumber for one of my rentals a couple months back because I knew they'd put them on the roof."

I smiled, but it made my gut hurt. "I'm sorry, too," I said. "I thought everyone knew."

"Well, not me; but now I do. Listen, I need 26 squares of three-tab white composition delivered on the roof sometime next week to another rental property. Can you do that?"

Long story short. There we were; we had taken steps to provide on-the-roof shingle delivery and we thought everyone knew. But, we weren't talking about it. Once it became old news to us, we didn't mention it much anymore. That's one thing that I know the monitors have done very well. We communicate through them that we repair windows and screens, match paint, cut keys, fill propane tanks, rent carpet cleaners and other items, deliver on the roof, of course, and other everyday stuff like that. The digital communication is constant and consistent. We won't make the mistake again of assuming that everyone knows everything we do. We offer specials and all the things that Kevin had originally suggested, too. I know for a fact that adding the flat screens has been a real good move for us.

Danny said that he read that the population of any given community turns over at a double digit rate every year. People move in, people move out. He made the point that if you don't continuously toot your own horn, so to speak, that you aren't doing everything you can to ensure your business stays healthy.

Here's another interesting thing he said: "Imagine walking in to a room that has four people in it, one in each corner. Three of those people are whispering or not talking at all. The fourth person is shouting." He then asked, "Which person do you see? Which corner do you turn to?"

I told him the answer was obvious and that I would look at the person who was shouting. He replied with one of his standard come-backs. "Bingo."

He went on to say that one of the opportunity check points of the Customer Asset Group, the 'Contact them' critical key, is to make your store noisier. In fact, he said to try to make your store the "noisiest" in the community. We came up with a lot of good ways to help us do that. We hold sidewalk sales, customer informational events, entertainment and food. Food always works. We sponsor local community organizations and make our parking lot available for car shows, girl scout cookie sales and even car washes. We changed the way we spent our marketing money. Some went to advertising and some went to marketing. I had always thought the two were the same, but through the Incremental Improvement system I learned there is an important distinction; Advertising involves featuring products at prices good enough to bring people in. Marketing, on the other hand, keeps our name in front of the community, aligns us with it and communicates things about our brand and our services.

By this time things were going good ... really good. All

four variables of the Opportunity Equation were up well above the goals we originally set using the online calculator. We were becoming successful!

***

One Thursday afternoon, I was feeling pretty good about myself, the store and what Kevin and the rest of our team were accomplishing. It occurred to me that I hadn't heard from Clancy since our last meeting, so I decided to initiate contact. (I told you I was feeling good.) I dialed his number. After a couple rings I heard, "Consumers' Bank, this is Gretchen, how may I direct your call?"

"Hi Gretchen, this is Charley Kern, is Clancy available?"

"Oh, hi Charley, I believe so, let me check."

It was a very short time before I heard Clancy's slow southern drawl. "Hello, Charley, so good to hear from you. How you been doin' anyway?"

"Hi Clancy. I'm doing great. I just wanted to check in. The last time we talked you asked about my budget, and I told you I was looking to do something different there. Anyway, I thought I'd give you a call and let you know that I got enrolled in a service that helps me with budgeting and goal setting, and it's really working well."

"That's great, Charley. Just great. I want to hear more about that some time. I've been seeing that you're doing much better. In fact, from what I see, it looks like you're doing great. Your deposits are up and you're developing a little cushion, aren't you?"

It felt good for him to notice our improvement. "Yeah, Kevin and I are thrilled about the ways things are going."

"Let me see now, Kevin is your assistant manager. Isn't that right?"

"Yes, that's right."

"Well, did I read that he and his wife just had a baby?"
"They sure did. He's been walking around like a zombie ever since."
Clancy laughed and replied. "I bet he's missing some sleep. A little one can sure do that, can't they? Now, remind me, did they have a little boy or a little girl?"
"A fine healthy boy. I don't remember how much he weighed, but they named him Kevin Jr. and they call him KJ."
"Well, isn't that wonderful? It's great to see additions like that in our community." As I listened I was thinking that Clancy epitomized my idea of a nice, older, southern gentleman.
"Well, tell me, Charley, do you think your store's improvement is because of the system you told me about the last time we met? I forget what you called it, but you were pretty excited about it."
"The Incremental Improvement System," I said.
"Oh, yes, that's right. Do you think that's the reason you're doing so much better?"
"It's not the only reason, but it's a big part of it. Once we understood the concept, we've built on it ourselves."
"Well obviously it's working. Charley, tell me, would that system work in other kinds of retail stores?"
I thought about it for a moment. "I don't see why not. It seems that all retail has basically the same challenges and opportunities. Heck, any place where you're offering a product or a service to people I think it would work and work pretty darn well.'
Clancy cleared his throat and then continued as if confiding, "I'll tell you what I'm thinking, Charley, and you can tell me no if you don't want to do this. But I want to run it by you anyway. We have quite a few businesses in our little town that could use a boost. Some of them really struggle and could use a hand up, you know? I'm very

impressed with the way you've turned your store around. Anyway, we have a meeting scheduled about 90 days from now where we're gonna bring in some other local businesses to see if we can answer any questions or help them in any way. Would you consider coming in and telling them about what you're doing and how you're approaching these changes? We'd be glad to pay you a little for your time."

I thought about taking the easy way out and telling him no. I've never been comfortable speaking in front of people. But then I considered where I'd have been without Danny's help and agreed to do it.

He told me he would contact me later with the schedule and other specifics. When I had mentioned the budget earlier, he expressed interest in learning about it, but he didn't say anything more, so I didn't either. Sleeping dog, and all that.

***

"So, he wants you to talk to these people and tell them what you've been doing at our store?" Julie asked.

"Yeah," I chuckled. "Crazy isn't it?"

"Not crazy, but kind of ironic, or something ... I don't know. On second thought, maybe it is crazy." She laughed easily and, as always, it made her even more beautiful.

"I'm kind of nervous about it," I said. "But I guess I'll just tell my story and if it can help anyone else, that'll be worth the stress."

Julie giggled again. "You'll do great. I know you will. Are you going to ask Kevin to go with you?"

"Nah, I don't think so. I thought about it, but we're short on help right now so I think I'll handle it myself and put less pressure on the store."

"You mentioned that you need to hire a couple people. Did

someone quit?"

"No. We're just busier than we were, and now that I've got a handle on budgeting, I think we can swing it. I'm going to hire two part-timers so we can manage payroll expenses more effectively. That'll give us more flexibility with scheduling."

"It seems like you always have a hard time finding anybody. What makes you think that you can find two people?" she asked.

"Well, I don't know for sure that we can. But the improvement system we're using has helped us identify ways to make our job openings look more appealing and to locate candidates from places we haven't looked before, so I'm optimistic."

"After you hire someone, how long does it take to get them up to speed? It seems like it would take quite a while before they'd be much help."

"It does take time, but Kevin's working on this training system that we're going to implement. It's really well thought-out. Gosh, promoting him has been such a good move. Anyway, he came up with this model that focuses on teaching new employees immediately the basic things they need to know to be initially productive. And then, from there, the training continues to build on that base and never really stops. It pushes for constant and continuous improvement. It's really cool."

"Sounds like it."

I was beginning to doze when Julie spoke again. "Have you seen KJ lately?"

"No. Kevin showed me a picture of him the other day. It looks like he's growing."

"Oh, my gosh, he is. And isn't he the cutest thing you ever saw? He's got those little round chubby cheeks and big blue eyes. It makes you just want to squeeze the stuffin' out of him. I just adore holding and cuddling him."

I didn't like the way this was going until Julie said as she reached over me to turn the light off. "You know, I was just thinking that maybe ....

Chapter 23

I believe it was the following Monday morning that Kevin stopped by my office and said, "Hey boss, you have time to talk?"

"Sure, Kevin. What's up?"

"I was reviewing our big Incremental Improvement System chart." He unrolled it. It was now covered with scribbled notes. "It seems like we've made really good progress with all of the asset groups except Facility."

"Yeah," I sighed and shrugged my shoulders before continuing. "Priorities and money, you know?"

"Sure, I get that, but I've been thinking maybe it's time we spend a little bit on the outside anyway. We don't have to make the building look brand new to make it stand out and be more appealing. That "Discovery-Based Retail" book said that the outside of a store is like the cover on a book. And it asked the question ... does the cover make you want to read the book? Or, in the case of a store, does the outside make you want to go inside?"

I knew he was right. I just wasn't sure about the timing. But, if I had learned anything at all on this adventure, it was that reaching further than you thought you could grasp could produce some pretty amazing results. "What did you have in mind?"

As I listened, I felt glad that he was comfortable bringing new ideas to me. "Nothing big, really. I was thinking maybe paint, change the color up a little bit, add some awnings over the windows and maybe new signs." His voice had an ascending tone which made it sound like he was asking a question.

He paused briefly and thumbed through his brief case again. "Look at these." He handed me a couple large pictures.

"Wow! Who did this?" I asked as I looked at the images. They were pictures of our store, but not the way it looked now. Someone had modified them to show how the store would look with Kevin's proposed changes. I was blown away.

He grinned from ear to ear. "You know Bryce Adams?"

"The high school teacher?"

"Yeah. He teaches computer out there. But he also teaches a night-course on PhotoShop at the JuCo. When he was in the other day I asked him if he could change a couple pictures of our store to show us how it would look if it were a different color and had some fresh signs on it. This is what he came up with. The awnings were his idea, and he picked the colors, too, but I think they look good."

"Wow. They look awesome." I said, shaking my head. "It all does. It's amazing that a bit of paint and canvas could change the looks of the place that much. I want to do it! We've got the paint. See what Bailey Brothers would charge us to spray it on. And then, who do you suppose we could call to get a price on awnings made to look like that?"

"Atkins Tent and Awning, I guess. You know, Bill Atkins' business out there on Elm Street? He comes in here a lot."

"Oh, sure. I know who you're talking about. OK, well, give Bill a call and arrange to show him these pictures. Have him give us a price. You're right; it's time we spruced this place up a bit."

"Did you like the size of the signs and where he has them placed?"

"Yeah, I do. But, I know there are some city regulations about sign sizes and how many you can have on a building. I'll call and check into that. We may have to change those up some, but after we know all the details, we'll contact a sign company."

"Sounds great," Kevin said. "I'm excited."

***

I don't remember the exact amount we spent refreshing the exterior, but it wasn't as much as I thought it would be. I can also tell you that whatever it was, it was a great investment. The new paint, signs and awnings made the store look great. In fact, it looked just like it had in the pictures Bruce made for us. The amount of comments we had from customers and the rest of the community after we completed the project was shocking.

I guess I didn't know how people viewed our store before, but we heard comments all the way from, "It looks awesome" ... "Glad to see you're investing in the community" ... "Looks like a different place" ... to my favorite: "We didn't even know you were here!" Really? They didn't know we were here? Well, anyway, comments are one thing, additional traffic and sales are different things entirely. Even though we had had steady growth since starting our push for incremental improvement we suddenly had a big spike. Let me tell you one thing I know for sure; *it's easier to manage your dollars when you have more dollars to manage.*

***

I was surprised one morning while working away in my office to see Clancy walk in.

"Knock, Knock."

"Hey Clancy, how are you? Come on in." (I can honestly say I was pleased to see him this time. That was quite a change!)

"Charley, your store looks wonderful. Just wonderful."

"Thanks, Clancy. I think it must have looked pretty bad before from the number of comments we've had," I said, smiling broadly.

"Well, I don't know about that, but people were talking about it, and I just wanted to come and see it for myself. Do you think it's been a good move for you?"

"Absolutely. Store traffic is really up. It has never been anywhere near what it is now, and I'm loving it."

"That's wonderful, Charley. Listen I don't want to take up much of your time, but remember that meeting I told you we were going to have for our local stores some time back?

I nodded and said, "Yeah, sure."

"Well, it's a week from Wednesday. We talked about you sharing with the group some of the things you're doing out here. Now that I've seen the latest, I'm even more excited about the possibility. Did you give it any more thought?"

"Yeah, I've thought about it, and I want to do it. But, I'm telling you up front, I'm not a polished speaker ... or a speaker of any kind for that matter.

Clancy chuckled. "Oh, my goodness, Charley. Don't worry yourself about that. We don't want a speaker. We just want you to share. You know, just visit with your friends in the community. We want them to hear your excitement and see what this push for improvement has done for you. Maybe they'll want to explore what something similar could do for them."

"Well, I'll try. I hope it adds something to your meeting."

"I'm sure it will, Charley. I'm sure it will! Like I said, it's a week from Wednesday at 11:30. We're meeting at the Knights of Columbus building. They made their meeting room available to us, so we'll have plenty of room. We're going to serve a little lunch and let everybody mingle a bit before we get started. There'll be a PA set up to make sure everyone can hear what's being said, and a projector if you want to use it."

I suddenly experienced a severe case of jelly spine. A PA system? A projector? Oh my lord, what have I gotten myself in to?

Breathe deeply, Charley. Confidence, Charlie.

"Sounds good, Clancy. I'll see you then."

***

Later that day when Kevin popped into my office I told him about committing to speak at the meeting for the bank. He thought my nerves and misgivings were pretty funny.

"What's the worst that could go wrong?" he said, laughing before continuing. "I suppose you could get up there and no words would come out. Or, you could get up there and suddenly realize you were so nervous you forgot to put your pants on. Or, you could forget everything we've done and just start stammering. Or ... "

I held up my traffic cop hand. "OK. Enough already. I came to you for support and this is the kind of respect I get?"

Kevin almost doubled over from his belly laugh and was gasping for air when he said, "I'm just kidding. You know that. You'll do great. You've got this."

I watched, silently, enjoying his performance. After a moment, and after he regained his composure, although he was still smiling, he said, "Hey boss, check out these numbers. Here on the left side are our original goals and this column over here, our latest numbers."

"Wow. That's awesome. We've blown our goals away haven't we?"

"Yeah, we sure have. So you know what that means don't you?"

"What? What do you mean?"

"We need to go back to that website and enter some bigger goals. We can't stop here. I think we've only scratched the surface of what we can accomplish."

"I agree, and I know there is one number I want to

change." I pulled a tablet, wrote a number on it, and pushed it across the table to Kevin.

"What's this?"

"It's your new salary starting the first of month."

"Are you serious? That's awesome, boss."

"Well, you deserve it. You've been key to our success, and I see great things in our future."

Kevin smiled slyly. "So, I guess that 'betting on the come' thing you told me about has paid off so far?"

***

The day for my presentation arrived, and I was exactly as I thought I would be; wild-eyed, crazy nervous. I made it to the Knights of Columbus about 11:15. There were already lots of people milling around in the meeting room. There were vendor booths set up showing various things, including a credit card processing company, an insurance representative and a succession planning company. People from the hospital and chamber of commerce were manning booths, too. There was information on the new school that was being proposed for the community. It was controversial so I'm not sure this was the best place to showcase it, but the bank was a strong supporter so it was easy to understand why they were doing it.

A light lunch of ham and turkey sandwiches, chips and cookies was served. There was tea and soft drinks, too, but I remember wishing that they were offering something a little stiffer.

Ross Johnson, another of the bank's vice-presidents, opened the meeting with greetings and "thank yous." He expressed excitement over the meeting and commented that he hoped it could become an annual event. He then turned the meeting over to Clancy.

Clancy approached the podium, cleared his throat and

began his usual slow, southern cadence, "I'm so glad you're all here with us today. It's so nice to have such a wonderful turnout. We have a nice program for you today. We're going to have a gentleman, Harry Conner, from Jenkins and Jenkins accounting service here in town bring you up to speed on some changes that will affect all of you come tax time."

There were moans and boos across the crowd. Clancy held his hand up before continuing, "Believe me, I feel the same way. We all do here at the bank, but it's something we've got to deal with so we'll arm ourselves with knowledge. That's the best we can do. We're also going to have Sabrina Thompson from the paper come up and tell you about a program they're putting together to help promote business in our town. But before we do any of that, I have persuaded Charley Kern to give you an overview about what he's been doing out at his store, Chard's Home Center. How many of you are familiar with his place?"

Many hands went up before he continued. "Well, if you've been by there or gone in there lately you've noticed a lot of changes over the last year or so. Anyway I asked Charley if he would share with you how he's been going about his improvements and he graciously agreed."

He turned to me and said, "Charley, come on up. And folks, please make Charley feel welcome."

I remember standing on noodle legs and walking up the steps to the stage in the front of the meeting room. As I approached the microphone and heard the group's applause I started contemplating how I could get out of this at the last moment. I could faint, maybe, or perhaps fake a trip and bang my head. Nah, it wouldn't work. Too late now, I thought, here goes nothing.

Clancy shook my hand and then walked off the stage. I glanced over the crowd, there must have been 100 people or more.

"Hello. Thank you for your applause and thank you, Clancy, for inviting me to be part of your meeting." I paused long enough to take a deep breath. (I had read somewhere that it would help.) "To tell you the truth, I feel kind of weird and a little inadequate to be up in front of you today offering advice. So, I've decided I'm not going to do that. What I'm going to do instead, is just tell you what we've been doing, how it came about, and let you know how it's impacted our business. Also, I want to let you know that if you have any questions, feel free to raise your hand and ask them. And, if something occurs to you after the meeting that you'd like to discuss further, catch me here or give me a call at the store. I'll help you any way I can."

I started at the beginning and included my chance stop at Miller Home Center, my subsequent friendship with Danny, Kevin's promotion and the shake-up of the crew. I also did a quick overview of the comprehensive process evaluations that we'd been undertaking. I explained the four variables of the Incremental Improvement Equation and how improving them had impacted our results. I tried to include all of the main points. I sincerely wanted to help others, if I could."

After I had learned that there was going to be a projector available, Julie helped me put together some slides for a short Power Point presentation. She learned how to do that in college, and she's pretty good at it. Anyway, the illustrations showed the equation, and the asset group charts, the critical keys we had identified and stuff like that. I also shared some data illustrating our improvements. After I had been at the podium for a few minutes, I started feeling pretty comfortable. That surprised me and to this day I don't know how it happened. Clancy had told me that he would like for me to talk about fifteen minutes or so, but when I tried to wrap up the discussion, questions just kept coming. It seemed that each one led to another. The group was clearly interested in what I had to say about improvement. Actually, the time passed quickly.

At this point, I glanced at Clancy, knowing I should have concluded several minutes earlier. He raised his eyebrows and shoulders, titled his head and rolled his hands to indicate for me to keep going as long as there was interest.

Another hand shot up.

I pointed to the gentleman and said, "Yes."

"Thanks for sharing; this has been real interesting."

"You're welcome. Thanks for listening." I smiled broadly and the group chuckled.

"This guy that you met, I think you said his name is Danny, did he come up with this system himself or did he learn it from someone else?"

I paused, taken off guard momentarily, because I honestly didn't know. Eventually I answered, "Funny thing. I never asked him. I assumed he came up with it himself, but he didn't say that." I paused again, shook my head slowly and finished, "I don't really know, but I'm going to find out."

There were a couple more questions and finally I saw Clancy glance at his watch, stand and approach the podium. "Thank you Charley. This has been so helpful and I think everyone has really enjoyed it. How about another hand for Charley? Didn't he do wonderful?"

I had learned already that "wonderful" was Clancy's favorite word. I was beginning to like it a lot, too. The group clapped enthusiastically.

I sat down in the front row of the audience and listened to the other presenters, but to tell you the truth, I can't remember a single word any of them said. I was basking in my success and relishing how far I had come.

***

When I arrived back at the store, Kevin was busy with customers but I read his face and knew that he was anxious to hear how my presentation had gone. I hadn't been in my office for more than 10 minutes when he walked in and sat down.

"So," he said. "Looks like you survived."

I laughed. "Yeah, it was nip and tuck there for a while, but I made it."

"So, tell me about it."

I shrugged, "It actually went pretty well. I was nervous at first, but I think I did OK. I kind of just told our story, what we've been doing and how it has helped us, and I found that it was easy to do."

"Were any of our competitors there?"

"No, I don't believe so. I had thought about that before I started, and I had made up my mind that if they were there, I'd still tell our story. But just the same, I'm glad they weren't."

Kevin chuckled. "Yeah, that would have been the pits, so I'm glad they weren't there, too."

"So what's going on around here?" I asked.

"We've been busy. People are still talking about the outside of the building, and we had three more people come in and say they didn't even know we were here."

I shook my head. "Weird."

Kevin smiled, "Yeah, but it's a good weird. Right? Hey, listen, I also called Danny to pick his brain a bit. I hope you don't mind."

"Mind?" I chuckled, "Of course not. Let's learn all we can from him. What were you asking him about?"

"Well, I was going back over our opportunity check points for the Products Asset Group and particularly the 'Price Them' Critical Key, and I noticed that when we were discussing pricing I had written down 'Communicate it.' I don't think we did anything about that and so I wondered if it was an oversight."

"And?"

"Yeah, it probably was. When I talked to Danny he said one thing that really made me think, though."

"What's that?"

"He said, 'You can change everything about your store, but until you tell somebody, you haven't really changed anything.'"

"That doesn't make much sense to me. You'd think people would see the changes," I said.

"That's what I said, too, at first. He said that regular customers might notice the changes and they might not. But people who are not your customers would definitely not know anything about the changes, whatever they were. That's why he said, you have to tell them."

"So, we should tell people that we think our prices are good?"

"Communicate it someway, yeah."

"So how did he propose we do that?"

"He gave me some ideas to get started. He mentioned putting price flags up on items, especially the ones we know we're very competitive on. He suggested having several on each aisle side. He said that they should say something like 'our everyday value price.' He thought it would be good idea for us to use "value" in our price communication. I remember him, or you saying ... or maybe I read it in one of those books that when perceived value exceeds price the sale takes place."

"I don't think it was me, chief. But, anyway, we could do that easy enough, I suppose, what else?"

"He said that when we lower a price on an item **for any reason** we should make a big deal about it by putting a 'New Lower Price' tag on it."

"You mean like the big blue store always brags that

they're 'rolling back prices?'"

"Yeah, I guess so. I'm thinking it would be exactly the same thing ... communicating lower prices."

I nodded and he glanced at his notes again. "Here's something he said, too. He said to make sure that all of the items on the main end caps, you know the ones near the front and the ones that flank the cash wrap, the most visible ones, feature low prices."

"Well, we always try to have good prices on all of our end cap items."

"Yeah, but he wasn't talking about *good* prices. What he meant was that if we have a drill that is regularly $150 on sale for $125, that would be a good price. But it wouldn't be a low price. He meant we should feature lower priced items on those end caps. Items that sell for $10 or less or even $5 or less would be better. He said it would be a powerful thing for customers to see low prices when they first walk in. It would subliminally communicate to them that we have low prices throughout the store."

I shrugged my shoulders. "Wouldn't cost anything to try it, I guess."

"That's what I thought. He also mentioned using something about price in a tag line."

"Tag line?"

"Yeah, you know a phrase to use in our advertising and marketing. He suggested something like, 'Get treated nice and a real good price at Chard's Home Center.'"

I chuckled. "That's not bad, is it?"

Kevin responded, "No, it's not bad at all. I don't know if there could be a better one, but I do understand his point. I've heard it said that if you say something loud enough and long enough, even if it's not completely true, people will begin to believe it."

"Yeah, I've heard that, too. And, if you listen to all of the political BS that's going on right now, I'm inclined to think so."

He laughed. "So what do you think?"

"You mean what do I think about his suggestions?"

He nodded.

"I think they're great. Let's try them. We're not talking about any big expense really. So, yeah, make it happen."

"Do you want to use that tag line in our ads?"

"Unless we can think of something better, and I ain't holding my breath on that one."

He chuckled, "Yeah me either. Boy that Danny really knows his stuff, doesn't he?"

"He seems to, for sure. Oh, by the way, you know what someone asked me at the presentation today?"

"I have no idea."

"He asked me if the Incremental Improvement System was Danny's brainchild or if he had learned it somewhere else. It had never occurred to me to ask. He never said, did he?"

Kevin moved his head from side to side. "Not that I remember, boss. I guess it wouldn't make any difference, would it?"

"No, it wouldn't, but I am curious. I've always just viewed him as this fountain of knowledge, and maybe I assumed he was the source. I don't know. You're right it doesn't matter, but I'm going to ask him someday anyway."

Kevin rose to leave as my phone began ringing. It was Julie.

"Hey Jewels, how's it going?"

"Good for me, but how about you? You're the one who made the big appearance today."

"It's going fine. The meeting was good. I think I did pretty well."

"I knew you would. You've got to tell me all about it when you get home. What time should I plan dinner, we're going to have a guest."

"A guest? Who?"

"It's a surprise. Will 6:30 work?"

"Yeah, that'll be fine. Do I know this person?"

"No, not yet. But you will. It's a surprise though and there will be no more questions or clues or rhymes, and I mean it. Anybody want a peanut?" she giggled.

I was curious, but I didn't ask for any more details.

"OK." I said, "See you soon."

Chapter 24

I walked into the house that night and it smelled amazing. I could tell from the garlic and other spices (mostly the garlic) that we were going to have Italian food. Julie wasn't in the kitchen, but the oven was warm and there was a pot of some kind of sauce simmering on the surface. As I made my way to the dining room, I thought: Wow, I don't know who our guest is, but Julie must really want to impress them. She was using the good China. At my house that just doesn't happen. The good China stays in the hutch, gets cleaned once in a blue moon, but otherwise never sees the light of day. There were wine glasses on the table, too and candles. Candles, are you kidding me? What the heck?

"Hey Jewels, where are you?"

"I'm up here," she called from upstairs. "I needed to change. I'll be down in a bit. Pour yourself a glass of wine."

"Ok. You want one, too, don't you?"

"No, I don't think so. I'll just have water."

Did I mention the music? She had music playing. It was soft, and someone more sensitive might have even thought it was romantic.

"Hi, Charley. Congratulations on your big day."

I turned around, saw her descending the stairs, and couldn't believe my eyes. "Julie, you look amazing. That dress is awesome. It's my favorite, and you make it look beautiful and vice-versa. OK. Spill the beans. Who the heck is coming to dinner?" I raised my eyebrows, wolf-whistled, flashed my best "sexy-man look" and then said, "on the second thought, how soon are they going to be here?"

"Charley, behave yourself." She feigned shock and pushed

me away.

I glanced at the table. "Hey, wait a minute. What's going on here? There are only two places set at the table. Did our guest cancel?"

She smiled again, "Nope, they're here."

I was confused.

"Where? What do you mean?"

She moved closer, reached for my hand, placed it on her stomach and said. "Right here." She smiled and waited.

I'm slow, but not that slow. "A baby?" I exclaimed, "Really? When?"

"The Dr. said she thought I was probably about three months along, so I guess six months or so."

The rest of the night was a blur. I wanted Julie to see I was excited, and I was, but I was also very apprehensive. Nope, check that, I was scared stiff. I didn't know a thing about raising babies. Julie told me that we'd grow into it, but I wasn't convinced. She said later that I told her all about the day's meeting that night, but I don't recall it at all. I guess I was in an altered state.

***

The next several weeks, while we continued our push for improvement, Kevin enjoyed making fun of my nervousness about our upcoming arrival. I observed that he and Rhonda had settled in fine with KJ, so I was becoming more confident that Julie and I would, too. But still, I was apprehensive. Julie seemed to take it all in stride. She did have a few "down days" thinking about not having her mom and dad around to support her and to enjoy the baby with us. Thankfully those days were few and fleeting.

At the store, we continued to get busier. We had extended

our Saturday hours, which was a great move. Between our efforts for margin improvement and the shift in the balance of contractor trade versus consumer trade our margin was better than I thought we could achieve. That having been said, we continued to use the Incremental Improvement System to look for additional opportunities. One day while I was walking through the store, I asked Kevin to join me in the paint department.

"You know," I said, "I don't think I'm ready to commit to remodeling the whole store, but I was just thinking that we could spruce up this department for starters. We could make it look like a paint store inside of our store. That would be kind of fun, wouldn't it?"

"You bet, boss. Did you have something in mind?" Kevin asked.

"I was thinking we could change the floor covering in the area. Maybe open up this center aisle around the color chip racks over here, do some spotlighting, use brighter colors. I don't know. Maybe some new signs."

"Sounds interesting. But, are you sure you don't want to just tackle the whole store?"

I let out a long sigh. "I'd like to, but I don't know. That would take a big commitment. I'd have to borrow money, and I don't know how the bank would view that. We've made great progress, but I don't know if Clancy would be open to something like that or not."

Kevin shrugged his shoulders, "I don't know either, but you'll never know if you don't ask."

I wrestled with the idea that night. I talked to Julie and expressed some concern about tackling a project like that with the baby coming and all.

She set me straight P.D.Q. "Charley don't you dare use our baby as an excuse for not doing what you think you need to do or want to do. That's not the way it's going to work, mister!"

Tell me how you really feel, I thought. But I was glad to have her support.
There was more to the conversation, but by that time, my brain was overloaded. I was excited and scared stiff at the same time. We had come so far but this would be an even bigger challenge. On the surface, however, it seemed that it would also be a greater opportunity.
That's how I found myself in Clancy's office the next morning.

***

"Charley, so good to see you," Clancy said as he extended his hand.
"Thanks, Clancy. It's good to see you, too." I said.
"Looks like you're still knocking 'em down out there. It's just wonderful to see how you've turned your store around."
I nodded. "It is pretty amazing to see how far we've come. I guess it surprises even me. Maybe mostly me. It's been hard work, but it's been fun, too."
"It's always fun to be successful, isn't it? That's just wonderful, Charley."
I didn't want to delay the purpose of my visit any longer so I said, "That's what brings me here today. I want our store to be even more successful."
"Well, I do, too. How can we help?"
"Do you remember when we spruced up the outside of the store a while back?"
"Yes, I do. It looks wonderful."
"Well, that's been a good move for us, and Kevin and I were talking. We think fixing up the inside would help just as much ... maybe more. But I couldn't do that without getting some kind of loan."
I held my breath. I didn't know what his reaction would

be, but I can tell you for certain that I didn't expect what followed.

"Have you put your figures and a pro forma together yet?"

"No. I wanted to visit with you first and ..."

Clancy interrupted me, "Well, the reason I'm asking is this; you're familiar with the old Save-On-Food building out on Highway 52 aren't you?"

"Yeah, they built a bigger building to the east of the old one..."

"Well, the guy who owns the old building is wanting to sell it and pretty badly too. I think he's got an attractive price on it. There's some ground to the west that comes with the building, too. When he talked to me about it, I immediately thought of you. In fact, it's ironic that you called, because I was going to call you later today."

Shut the front door! I thought.

"I don't know what to say," I said, "I'm blown away. My knee-jerk reaction is that the building would make a good home center, but I'll have to do some homework on that idea."

Clancy laughed. "Oh my. Yes, you will. But let me tell you this: If you want to explore relocating, that's great. If you decide you'd rather remodel your building, we'll work with you there, too. You've proved to me that you can handle either project. Remember though, with what he's asking for the property, we'd use it for security and be able to extend some additional capital to help get the building ready and cover relocation expenses. I told you already that it's a really good price. We'd need to act quickly if you decide you want to do it."

"Do you think my current building would be sellable?"

"Oh, yes. I know it would. In fact, if you decide that's what you want to do, I've got a couple people I'll call that I think may be interested."

***

After discussing Clancy's proposal with Julie that night, I walked into the store the next morning. I relayed the story to Kevin and he was "off the walls" excited. I tried to temper his enthusiasm enough to get him to help me think clearly.

"But, aren't you excited?" Kevin asked.

"Yeah, I'm excited, but I'm apprehensive, too. We've got things going pretty good here now and I don't want to jeopardize that."

"I get that, but we can go through the process again and accomplish the same thing on a different scale. The difference would be the size of the building. It's got to be twice as big."

"I would guess so, but is that a good thing or a bad thing? That's what we need to determine."

"Have you told Danny?" he asked.

"No, I thought we might do that together this morning and see what he suggests."

"Let's do. I'll be anxious to see what he says."

After a few more minutes of conversation I dialed Danny's cell phone number and put him on the speaker.

Danny answered quickly, "Hey, Charlie. What's up, my man?"

"Morning, Danny. Kevin and I are sitting here discussing an opportunity that we've been given."

I recounted my conversation with Clancy and brought him up to speed on the things that Kevin and I had already discussed.

"Well, now, that's pretty danged exciting. You're going to go for it aren't you?"

"I want to explore it, but honestly I don't even know where to begin," I said.

"Well, start with the Facility Asset Group of the

Incremental Improvement System. The first Critical Key is Choose it, and it's all about making sense of a location. That's where I'd start, anyway."

"Hey, that reminds me, there's something Kevin and I have wanted to ask you. Is the Incremental Improvement System your idea? Did you come up with it?"

Danny laughed heartily. "Oh, my lord no. Did you think that I did?"

"You didn't tell us otherwise," I said.

"You didn't ask, my man."

I paused realizing he was right but not knowing how I felt about it.

He eventually spoke sounding somewhat sheepish. "I guess I knew you thought that I did. And, to tell you the truth, I kind of enjoyed that. I liked helping you, and you guys helped me when you started catching on and expanding the ideas. So, I figured it was a win-win. But anyway, no, it wasn't my idea. Sorry, if I mislead you. It's all from a book titled "Stores on Fire," and subtitled "The Workbook." There's another book that has the same title, but a different subtitle. It's called "Stores of Fire" "A Retailer's Story," I guess they're intended to be a set."

For a second I was a little pissed that Danny hadn't told me. But it lasted only a bit. It was still true that we owed most of our success to him and his coaching.

I asked, "So, have you read the other one, too? The story?"

"Read it, heck. I was born in it and so were you guys."

"Uh?"

"Oh, forget it. Bad joke. Anyway, if I were you, I'd start with the Facility section of the work book to help guide you through your decision. It has great ideas about presentation, too, so whether you move to the new building or stay where you are, you need the work book."

"Where did you buy it?" I asked.

"Got mine from Amazon. I don't know where else it's

available, but you can get it there for sure."

.

Chapter 25

It's been great sharing my experiences with you. I've got to get going soon, but I'd like to finish my story before I do. So, anyway, after the conversation with Danny that day, I ordered both of the Stores on Fire books. I read "A Retailer's Story" first and it gave me the strangest feeling. It felt as if I had lived through it all myself. I know ... weird, right?

I learned a lot from it, but Danny said that the "The Workbook" had become his reference for improving his store, and now it has become that for us, too.

We followed the steps outlined in The Workbook for our evaluation of the new site. During the process we also learned that there are six factors that produce gravitational pull for a retail store. They are called the 6 Ps of differentiation. They are; 1. Proximity, 2. People, 3. Presentation, 4. Products, 5. Pricing, and 6. Promotion. These attributes are important because retail pull determines a store's ability to pull customers through space and unto itself. That ability is critical in determining the success of any store. Of the six attributes Proximity is usually the most important. Proximity, in this case, refers to a store's physical location in relationship to concentrations of people. It also considers, ingress/egress, visibility and nearness to other retail stores. Shoppers often follow the path of least resistance and default to the closest source for their purchases. So position your store near concentrations of population, or choose a location with high exposure and you already have advantages.

The new site had good location. It was in a thriving shopping area. The parking lot of the empty building was big and bordered the parking lot of the one that had replaced it. The new grocery store had amazing traffic. We did highway traffic studies on the new site and contrasted them against the same data for the old store. We learned that by relocating we would have five and a half times more vehicles pass by our store every day. The new site set on an intersection with stop lights. It would be no problem for people to get in and out of the parking area, and the lights would also force people to slow down and notice our store

As the "The Workbook" suggested, we ordered demographic studies for the area too. The Retail Gap study that the workbook recommended indicated that there was a lot of business available for our store type. Using the Profit Explorer we put together different scenarios based on what we found during our exploration. We incorporated those numbers into our pro forma and prepared it for Clancy. We didn't have to wait long for an answer. Within a few weeks we had signed papers and were preparing for the big move. We compared the cost of moving our store fixtures with putting up some new ones in the new location. Well, actually, they weren't brand new, but they looked new and they were new to us. We opted to go that way. It allowed us to stay in business at the old location as long as possible. When it came time for the move we did most of it over a weekend. Several people from the community volunteered to help. We contracted with our hardware supplier for some help, too. Considering the size of the project, the move was incredibly smooth.

We used the same designers for our new store that Danny had used. Turns out they were the same guys who wrote Discovery-Based Retail and a few other books, too. They've spent their careers in this industry and their knowledge proved helpful. They were innovative and made great suggestions. You would see similarities to Danny's store, but it's unique as well. We love it and more importantly customers do, too.

That all happened a little over a year ago and we've been in the new building for eight months now. It's been challenging but very rewarding. Our sales are about three times what they were when we first initiated our improvement processes. As we hired more people, I named Kevin store manager; promoted him from assistant. I never make a decision about the store without his input. We are currently grooming Terrance for more responsibilities. Kevin and I still talk regularly about expansion. We have developed a five-year and a 10-year plan which includes additional stores. We have discussed a couple of adjacent communities that we think our model would fit nicely. What once seemed like "pipe dream" possibilities now feels tangible and there for the taking. Once in a while I open that folder with the "before" pictures of my old store. It's really gratifying to see how far we've come.

Julie and I have a beautiful and healthy little girl. We named her Melindy. Julie wanted to name her after her mother, but give her a unique name, too, so that's what we came up with. Now that the store is doing better, Julie has closed her shop, at least temporarily, and is focusing on being a mother. KJ is growing like a weed, too. Once in a while Rhonda drops by the store with him. He's a bundle of energy and kind of a one-boy "wrecking committee."

Kevin and I still talk to Danny once in a while, but not as often as we did. Like us, he's busy. He opened a second location in an adjacent town and it's doing very well. But, I think the main reason we don't hear much from him anymore is that he has a lady friend that keeps him pretty busy. The last time we talked I asked him if he was hearing wedding bells, and he said that whenever he does, he sticks his fingers in his ears until it goes away. Go figure. Anyway, I learned a lot from Danny and my chance encounter. Now I truly feel I have one of those "Stores on Fire."

Stores on Fire

Epilogue

Just in case you didn't realize it before, this book is a work of fiction. Charley, Danny, Kevin and the others exist only in my mind ... and now, of course, in these written words. The situations these characters faced may not be a lot different from ones you're dealing with today. I can tell you for certain that they are similar to situations that Gary and I have encountered while helping stores with our company, Discovery Retail Group. We have been assisting people build better operations for well over 10 years now. Buy *Stores on Fire "The Workbook"* if you haven't already. It will help you become more profitable. Of that, I am sure. It has actionable *opportunity check points* listed for the *Critical Keys* in each of the four asset groups. Will you have the crazy success that Charley experienced? Perhaps not; but on the other hand, your success may be even greater. At the very least, it will change the way you view your store and the possibilities that the future holds. I'm confident of that.

There's a great line in an old movie called Tombstone. The Doc Holiday character played by Val Kilmer comes to the aid of his friends several times by proclaiming "I'll be your huckleberry." (I have no idea what it meant, but it was cool and it always let his friends know that they could count on him.) In our story, fictional Danny helped fictional Charley, using the real *Increment Improvement System* that we created. It could help your store, too, and although, perhaps we can't "be your huckleberry," we can "be your Danny." You can learn the system through the books, but we're also available for onsite visits. After a day or two in your store we can make recommendations that will help improve your operation. I say that not because we're smarter than you, but because we'll bring fresh, *experienced* perspectives to your operation by viewing it through new eyes and the Incremental Improvement System.

The Profit Explorer is real, too. You can learn more about it on our website, discoveryretailgroup.com. Simply stated, The Profit Explorer is a dynamic budgeting, goal setting and coaching service. It can give you a better handle on your operation and help move your store to greater profitability.

Thanks for reading this book. We appreciate it. If you enjoyed it and think others might enjoy it as well, please take a few minutes to review it on Amazon. That would help us greatly. Thanks in advance for that.

Phil Mitchell and Gary Petz

Made in the USA
Monee, IL
20 September 2022